SPANISH-ENGLISH DICTIONARY OF GARDENING AND LANDSCAPING

EL DICCIONARIO ESPAÑOL-INGLÉS DE JARDINERÍA Y PAISAJISMO

Spanish-English Dictionary of Gardening and Landscaping

El Diccionario Español-Inglés de Jardinería y Paisajismo

Compiled and edited by Jay Miskowiec

ALIFORM PUBLISHING

Minneapolis   Oaxaca

ALIFORM PUBLISHING
aliformgroup@gmail.com   www.facebook.com/
aliformpublishing

Aliform Publishing's editorial offices are located at
Earthquake Arts
San Pablo Etla, Oaxaca, México
Please direct all communication to aliformgroup@gmail.
com

Layout and design by Carolyn Borgen
Cover photo by Lourdes Cué:
Alcatraces y girasoles, Casa Tobalá

Set in Times New Roman

ISBN 978-0-9822784-8-2

Aliform Publishing

Table of Contents

ENGLISH/SPANISH

INGLÉS/ESPAÑOL

FLOWERS, PLANTS, SHRUBS
FLORES, PLANTAS, ARBUSTOS

A
Ajuga. Ajuga.
Allysum. Aliso.
Amaryllis. Amarilis.
Ambrosia. Ambrosia.
Anemone. Anémona.
Annual. Anual.
Antirrhinum. Antirrino, boca de león o dragón.
Arum. Aro, jaro, yaro.
Asclepia. Asclepia.
Aster. Áster.
Azalea. Azalea.

B
Bamboo. Bambú, carrizo.
Begonia. Begonia.
Bellflower. Campanula.
Bird of Paradise. Ave de paraíso.
Bloodroot. Sanguinaria.
Bloom. Flor, floración.
> **To bloom.** Florecer.

Bluebonnet. Aciano, altramuz azul.
Bluebell. Campanilla, campánula.
Bluestem. Tallo azul.
Bluet. Aciano.
Bougainvillea. Buganvilla, trinitaria.
Box shrub. Seto de boj.
Bract. Bráctea.
Bromeliad. Bromelia.
Broom. Retama.
Buckeye. Castaño de Indias.

4

Buckthorn. Rhamnus.
Bud. Capullo.
   To bud. Brotar.
Bugleweed. Menta de lobo.
Bulb. Bulbo.
Bulrush. Espadaña, enea.
Burr plant. Lapa.
Bush. Arbusto, mata, matorral.
Buttercup. Botón de oro.

C
Cactus. Cacto, cactus.
Calathea. Calatea.
Calceolaria. Calceolaria.
Calyx. Cáliz.
Camellia. Camelia.
Cane. Caña.
Cardoon. Cardo.
Carnation. Clavel.
Cassia. Casia.
Castor oil plant. Ricino.
Cattail. Totora, espadaña.
Cenizo. Cenizo, ceniza.
Chaparral. Chaparral.
Chokeberry. Aronia.
Chrysanthemum. Crisantemo.
Cineraria. Cineraria.
Clematis. Clemátide.
Climber. Planta trepadora, enredadera.
Clover. Trébol.
Cockscomb, cock's comb, coxcomb. Cresta de gallo, moco de pavo.
Coleus. Cóleo.
Columbine. Aguileña, copa de rey.
Corm. Bulbo.

Cornel. Cornejo.
Coneflower. Equinácea.
Cornflower. Aciano.
Cotton. Algodón.
Cowslip. Prímula, primavera.
Creeper. Planta trepadora, enredadera.
Creosote bush. Creosota.
Crocus. Azafrán, croco.
Croton. Croton.
Crown. Corona.
Culm. Culmo.
Cultivar. Cultivar (v.), variedad (n.).
Cyclamen. Ciclamen, ciclamino.

D
Daffodil. Narciso.
Dahlia. Dalia.
Daisy. Margarita.
Dandelion. Diente de león.
Daphne. Daphne.
Delphinium. Delfinio.
Dianthus. Clavel, clavelina.
Dicentra. Corazón sagrante, maíz de ardilla.
Dock. Acedera.
Dogbane. Adelfa.
Dracaena. Dracaena.
Duckweed. Lenteja de agua.
Dwarf. Enano, -a.

E
Elephant's ears. Bergenia.
Epiphyte. Epifita.
    Epiphytic. Epifítico, -a.
Evolvulus. Daze azul, evólvulo.
Exotico. Exótico, -a.

F

Fan. Follaje, frondosidad.
Fern. Helecho.
>**Beech fern.** Helecho de haya largo o estrecho.
>**Hard fern.** Lonchite.
>**Maidenhair.** Culantrillo, adianto.
>**Male fern.** Helecho macho, dentabrón.
>**Royal fern.** Helecho real.

Ficus. Ficus.
Fireweed. Laurel de San Antonio.
Flax. Lino.
Flower. Flor.
Forb. Forbe.
Forget-me-not. Nomeolvides.
Fountain grass. Pasto pennisetum.
Foxglove. Digital, dedalera.
Freesia. Fresia.
Frond. Fronda, hoja de helecho o palmera.
Fuchsia. Fucsia.

G

Gardenia. Gardenia.
Garland. Guirnalda.
Gentian. Genciana.
Genus. Génio.
Geranium. Geranio.
Ginger. Jengibre.
Gladiola. Gladiola, gladiolo.
Goldenrod. Vara de oro, plumero amarillo.
Grass. Pasto.
>**Grass blade.** Brizna.
>**Grassy.** Herboso, -a; pastoso, -a.

Gypsophila. Gisófila, nube de novia.

H

Habitat. Hábitat.

Hackberry. Celtis.

Harebell. Campanilla.

Hawthorn. Majuelo, espino blanco.

Heather. Brezo.

Hedge. Seto.

> **Hedgerow.** Seto vivo o verde.

Heliotrope. Heliotropo.

Hemlock. Cicuta, etusa.

Hemp. Marijuana.

Herbaceous. Herbáceo, -a.

Hibiscus. Hibisco.

Hippeastrum. Hippeastrum.

Holly. Acebo.

Hollyhock. Malva arbórea, real o rósea; malvarrosa.

Honeysuckle. Madreselva.

> **Trumpet honeysuckle.** Madreselva de trompeta o de coral.

Hosta. Hosta.

Houseplant. Planta de interior.

Hyacinth. Jacinto.

> **Wild or Wood hyacinth.** Jacinto silvestre.

Hybrid. Híbrido.

Hydrangea. Hortensia.

I

Impatiens. Alegría de la casa.

Indigo. Indigo.

Intrusive. Intrusivo, -a.

Iris. Iris.

Ivy. Hiedra, yedra.

J

Jasmine, jessamine. Jazmín.

Jimsomweed. Estramonio.

Kudzu. Vid kudzu.

L
Lady's slipper. Zapatilla de dama.
Lantana. Lantana.
Larkspur. Consuelda, espuela de caballero.
Leaf. Hoja.
    Fleshy leaf or rib of an agave. Penca.
Leaflet. Folíolo, foliolo.
Liana. Liana.
Lichen. Liquen.
Lilac. Lila (flower), lilo (shrub).
Lily. Azucena, lirio.
    Calla lily. Alcatraz.
    Tiger lily. Lirio atigrado.
    Waterlily. Lirio acuático, nenúfar.
Linseed. Linaza.
Lobelia. Lobelia.
Lupin. Lupinus, altramuz.
    White lupin. Altramuz.
Lyreflower. Corazón sangrante.

M
Marguerite. Margarita.
Marigold. Caléndula.
Marsh grass. Juncia, junco.
Meristem. Meristemo.
Mesquite. Mesquite.
Milkweed. Algondoncillo.
Mimosa. Mimosa.
Mondo grass. Césped ornamental.
Morning glory. Campanillas, campanitas, enredadera.
Moss. Musgo.
Mulberry. Morera.
Mum. Crisantemo.
Myrtle. Mirto, arrayán.

Bog myrtle. Mirto de Brabante o de turbera.
Crape or crepe myrtle. Lagerstromia.

N
Narcissus. Narciso.
Nasturtium. Capuchina, taco de reina.
Native. Nativo, -a.
Nettle. Ortiga.
Nonintrusive. No intrusive, -a.

O
Oleander. Adelfa.
Orchid. Orquídea.

P
Panicle. Racimo de flores, panícula, panoja.
Pansy. Pensamiento.
Passion flower. Pasionaria.
Patient Lucy. Alegría de la casa.
Pedicel. Pedúnculo.
Pelargonium. Pelargonio.
Peony. Peonía.
Peperomia. Peperomia, pimienta.
Perennial. Perenne.
Periwinkle. Hierba doncella, vincapervinca.
Petal. Pétalo.
Petiole. Peciolo.
Petunia. Petunia.
Phlox. Flox.
Phorb. Forbe.
Plant. Planta.
Plume. Pluma.
　　Plumage. Plumaje.
Poinsettia. Nochebuena, flor de Pascua.
Poison ivy. Hiedra venenosa.

Poison oak. Roble venenosa.
Poisonwood. Zumaque venenosa.
Polyanthus. Prímula, primavera.
Polypody. Polipodio.
    Polypodeous. Polipodiacio,-a.
Poppy. Amapola.
Potato vine. Falso jazmín, jazmín solano.
Primrose, primula. Prímula, primavera.
Privet. Ligustro, alheña, aligustre.
Purslane. Portulaca, verdolaga.

Q
Queen Anne's lace. Zanahoria salvaje.
Quickthorn. Majuelo.

R
Ragwort. Hierba cana.
Ranunculus. Ranúnculo.
Reed. Junco.
Rhododendrun. Rododendro, azalea.
Rhizome. Risoma.
Root. Raíz.
Rose. Rosa.
    Tea rose. Rosa té.
Rose laurel. Adelfa.
Runner. Estolón.
Rush. Junco.
Rye. Centeno.

S
Safflower. Alazor, cártamo.
Salsolaceous. Salsolaceo, -a.
    Salsoginus. Salsogineo, -a.
Salvia. Salvia.
Scion. Vástigo, esqueje.

Sedge. Juncia, junco.
Seed. Semilla.
Seed pod. Vaina.
Seedling. Planta de semillero, plantón.
Senna. Sen, sena.
Sepal. Sépalo.
Shoot. Brote, retoño.
Shrub. Arbusto, matorral.
Skunk cabbage (Lysichiton americanus). Col de mofeta occidental o amarillo. (Symplocartus foetidus). Col de mofeta oriental, col de los prados o pantanos.
Snapdragon. Boca de dragón, conejito.
Snowdrop. Campanilla de invierno.
Soaptree. Palmilla, sota.
Sod. Césped, terrón.
Sphagnum moss. Esfagno.
Spathe. Espata.
Spikenard. Nardo.
Spore. Espora.
Sprout. Brote.
Spurge. Euforbio, euforbia.
Stalk. Tallo.
Star of Bethlehem. Estrella de belén.
Stem. Tallo.
Succulent. Suculente.
Sucker. Retoño.
Sumac. Zumaque.
Sunflower. Girasol, tornasol, mirabel, mirasol.
Sunpatiens. Alegría.
Sweet pea. Guisante de olor, alverjilla.
Switchgrass. Pasto varilla.

T
Tallo azul. Bluestem.

Tansy. Atanasia, hierba de Santa María o lombriguera.
Thicket. Matorral.
Thistle. Cardo.
Tobacco. Tabaco.
Trefoil. Trébol, trifolio.
Trillium. Trilio, trillium.
Trumpet vine. Enredadera de trompeta.
Tulip. Tulipán.
Tumbleweed. Planta rodadora o corredora.
Tussock. Mata de hierba.

V
Variety. Variedad.
Venus flytrap. Dionaea atrapamoscas, dionaea muscipula.
Verbena. Verbena.
Vetch. Algarroba.
Vinca. Vincapervinca.
Vine. Vid (grapes), parra, enredadera.
Violet. Violeta.

W
Wand. Varita.
Weed. Maleza, mala hierba.
Weigela. Veigela, veigelia.
Wildflower. Flor silvestre.
Wilding. Planta salvaje.
Wisteria. Glicinia.
Witch hazel. Avellano de bruja, escoba de bruja.
Wood sorrel. Oca.
Woody (thick, tough). Leñoso, -a.
Wreath. Corona de flores, guirnalda.

Y
Yarrow. Milenrama, aquilea.

Z
Zinnia. Zinnia.

CACTI AND SUCCULENTS
CACTUS Y SUCULENTES

A
Agave. Agave.
Aloe. Áloe.

B
Ball cactus. Cactus bola, cholla.
Barrel cactus. Biznaga.
Beaver tail cactus. Cola de castor.
Bird's nest cactus. Cacto nido de pájaro.
Bishop's cap. Cactus Estrella.
Bishop's miter. Capa de obispo, astrofito.
Brain cactus. Pedo de perro.
Branched pencil cholla. Cholla lápiz.
Bunny ear cactus. Alas de ángel, cactus de lunares, orejas de conejo.
Button cactus. Cacto de botón.

C
Cabera cactus. Cacto cabeza blanca.
Cactus. Cactus.
Calico cactus. Cactus de erizo.
Candelabra. Candelabra.
Candy barrel cactus. Biznaga de agua, cacto de barril.
Century plant. Jarcia.
Cholla. Cholla.

L
Lindsay's hedgehog. Cacto de Lindsay.
Living rock. Roca viviente.

M
Maguey. Maguey.

O
Ocotillo. Ocotillo.
Orchid cactus. Cactus orquídea.

P
Peyote. Peyote.
Prickly pear. Nopal.

S
Saguaro. Saguaro, órgano.
Succulent. Suculente.

T
Teddy-bear cholla. Cholla de oso teddy.
Thanksgiving cactus. Cactus de Navidad.

GENERA OF CACTI AND SUCCULENTS
GÉNEROS DE CACTUS Y SUCULENTES

<u>Cacti</u>

Aporocactus
Ariocarpus.
Astrophytum
Cephalocerus
Cereus
Cleistocactus
Copiapoa
Coryphantha
Echinocactus
Echinocereus
Echinopsis
Epiphyllum
Espostoa
Ferocactus
Gymnocalycium
Haageocereus
Hildewinteria
Lobivia
Lophophora
Mammillaria
Matucana
Melocactus
Neobuxbaumia
Neoporteria
Notocactus
Opuntia
Oreocerus
Pachycerus
Parodia
Pilosocereus

Rebutia
Rhipsalis
Sansevieria
Schlumbergia
Stenocactus
Stenocerus
Sulcorebutia
Thelocactus
Trichocerus
Turbinicarpus
Uebelamannia

Succulents

Adenium
Adromischus
Aeonium
Agave
Aichryson
Aloe
Aloinopsis
Ceropegiea
Conophytum
Cotyledon
Crassula
Dasylirion
Dudleya
Echeveria
Euphorbia
Faucaria
Gasteria
Gibbaeum
Greenovia
Haworthia
Hoya
Huernia

Jatropha
Kalanchoe
Lampranthus
Lithops
Nolina
Pachyphtum
Pachypodium
Pedilanthus
Piaranthus
Pleiospilos
Sansevieria
Sedum
Sempervivum
Senecio
Stomatium
Titanopsis
Trichodiadema
Tylecodon
Yucca

FRUITS AND VEGETABLES
FRUTAS Y VEGETALES

A
Achene. Aquenio.
Apple. Manzana.
Artichoke. Alcachofa.
Arugula. Arúgula.
Asparagus. Espárrago.
Aubergine. Berenjena.

B
Banana. Plátano, banana.
Bean. Frijol.
    Black bean. Frijol negro.
    Butter bean, Lima bean. Haba de lima.
    Navy bean, white bean. Aluvia.
    Soybean. Soya.
    Wax bean. Haba amarilla de cera, frijol de cera.
Beet. Betabel.
Berry. Baya.
Blackberry. Zarzamora, mora.
Blueberry. Arándano azul, mora azul.
Broccoli. Brócol, broccoli.
Brussel sprout. Col de Brusela.

C
Cabbage. Col.
Cantaloupe. Melón, cantalupo.
Capsicum. Pimiento.
Carrot. Zanahoria.
Cauliflower. Coliflor.
Celery. Apio.
Chard. Acelga.
Chicory. Endibia, endivia.

Chicory root. Achicoria.
Chili pepper. Chile.
Coconut. Coco.
Collard. Berza.
Coffee bush. Cafeto.
Corn. Maíz.
Courgette. Calabacita, calabacín.
Cranberry. Arándano.
Cress. Berro.
Cucumber. Pepino.

E
Eggplant. Berenjena.
Endive. Endibia, endivia.

F
Fig. Higo.
French bean. Elote, alubia verde.
Fruit. Fruta.

G
Gourd. Calabaza.
Grape. Uva.
Grapefruit. Pomelo, toronja.
Green bean. Ejote.
Guava. Guayaba.

H
Heirloom (e.g. heirloom tomato). Reliquia, típica, tradicional.
Honeydew melón. Melón chino.
Hybrid. Híbrido.

K
Kale. Col risado, berza.
Kernel. Grano.

Kiwi. Kiwi.
Kohlrabi. Colirrábano.

L
Leek. Poro, puerro.
Legume. Legumbre.
Lemon. Limón.
Lettuce. Lechuga.
Lime. Lima, limón verde.
Loquat. Níspera.
Lupin bean. Altramuz.

M
Mandarin orange. Mandarina, tangerina.
Marrow. Calabacita, calabacín.
Medlar. Níspera.
Melon. Melón, cantalopo.
Mulberry. Mora.
Mushroom. Champiñon, hongo.
Muskmelon. Cantalupo.

N
Nectarine. Nectarina, pavía.

O
Okra. Angu, ocra.
Onion. Cebolla.
Orange. Naranja.

P
Parsnip. Chirivía, pastinaco, nabo.
Passion fruit. Maracuyá, granada china.
Pea. Chícharo.
Pepper. Pimiento.
    Banana pepper. Pimiento amarillo.
    Bell pepper. Pimiento.

Cherry pepper. Pimiento rojo.
Sweet pepper. Pimiento.
Pineapple. Piña.
Peach. Durazno.
Pear. Pera.
Plum. Ciruela.
Potato. Papa.
Pumpkin. Calabaza.

Q
Quince. Membrillo.

R
Radish. Rábano.
Raspberry. Frambuesa.
Rhizome. Rizoma.
Rhubarb. Ruibarbo.
Ripe. Maduro, -a.
    To ripen. Madurar.
Rutabega. Naba.

S
Salisfy. Escorzonera.
Seed. Semilla.
Shallot. Chalota, chalote.
Spinach. Espinaca.
Squash. Calabacita.
Spore. Espora.
Strawberry. Fresa.
Sweet corn. Maíz dulce.
Sweet potato. Camote.

T
Tangerine. Mandarina, tangerina.
Tomato. Jitomate.
    Cherry tomato. Tomatito cherry.

Green tomato. Tomatillo.
Tuber. Tubérculo.
Turnip. Nabo.

V
Vegetable. Vegetal.
Watercress. Berro.
Watermelon. Sandía.

Y
Yam. Camote.
Yucca. Yuca.

Z
Zucchini. Calabacita.

HERBS/HIERBAS

A
Amaranth. Amaranto.
Anise. Anís.

B
Basil. Albahaca.
Bay leaf. Hoja de laurel.
Borage. Borraja.

C
Chervil. Perifollo.
Chamomile. Manzanilla.
Chives. Cebolleta, cebollino.
Cilantro. Cilantro.
Citronella. Hierba o zacate de limón, limoncillo, hierba luisa.
Clove. Clavo.

D
Dill. Eneldo, abesón.

F
Fennel. Hinojo.
Feverfew. Matricaria, santa maría.

G
Garlic. Ajo.

H
Herb. Hierba.
Hyssop. Hisopo.

L
Lavender. Lavanda.

Lemon verbena. Hierba luisa.

M
Marjoram. Mejorana.
Mint. Menta.
Mustard. Mostaza.

O
Oregano. Oregano.

P
Parsley. Perejil.

R
Rosemary. Romero.

S
Sage. Salvia.
Savory. Ajedrea.
Sorrel. Acedera, agrilla.
Spearmint. Hierbabuena.

T
Tarragon. Estragón.
Thyme. Tomillo.

W
Woodruff. Asperilla, galio.

TREES/ÁRBOLES

A
Acacia. Acacia.
Alder. Aliso.
Almond. Almendro.
Apple tree. Manzano.
Ash. Fresno.
Aspen. Álamo temblón.

B
Balsa. Balso.
Banana tree. Platanero, banano.
Bark. Corteza.
Basswood. Tilo.
Beech. Haya.
Bergamot. Bergamota.
Birch. Abedul.
Boxwood. Boj, boje, setos.
Branch. Rama.
Brazilwood. Palo de Brasil, palo Brasil, palo de agua.

C
Carob tree. Algarroba.
Cashew tree. Acajú, anacardo marañón.
Cassia. Casia.
Cedar. Cedro.
Ceiba. Ceiba.
Cherry tree. Cerezo.
Chestnut tree. Castaño.
Cinnemon. Canela.
Citrus. Cítrico (n.), cítrico, -a (adj.).
Coconut tree. Cocotero.
Conifer. Conífera.
    Coniferous. Conífero, -a.

Cork tree. Alcornoque.
Crab apple. Manzana silvestre.
Cypress. Ciprés.

D
Deciduous. Caducifolio, -a.
Dogwood. Cornejo.
Ebony. Ébono.
Elderberry. Saúco, sabuco.

E
Elm. Olmo.
Evergreen. Árbol de hoja perenne (n.), de hoja perenne (adj.)

F
Eucaluptus. Eucalipto.
Feijoa. Feijoa.
Fig tree. Higuera.
Fir. Abeto, álamo.
    Balsam fir. Abeto balsámico.
    Silver or white fir. Abeto blanco.

G
Grapefruit tree. Pomelo.
Guava tree. Guayabo.

H
Hardwood. Árbol de hojas caducas.
Hazel or hazelnut tree. Avellano.
Hickory tree. Nogal americano, pacana.
Hornbeam. Carpe.

J
Jacaranda. Jacarandá.
Joshua tree. Árbol Joshua.

Juniper. Junipero.

K
Kapok tree. Miraguano.
Kumquat tree. Quinito.

L
Larch. Alerce, lárice.
Laurel. Laurel.
Lemon tree. Limonero.
Limb. Rama.
Lime tree. Limero.
Linden. Tilo.
Locust. Acacia blanca, algarrobo, robinia.
Loquat tree. Níspero.

M
Mahogany. Caoba.
Magnolia. Magnolia.
Mallow. Malva.
Mangrove. Manglar.
Maple. Arce.
Medlar. Níspero.
Mulberry tree. Moral.

O
Oak. Roble, encino.
    Live oak. Roble siempre verde.
    Red oak. Roble americano, boreal, rojo o rojo del norte.
    Scrub oak. Encinillo.
    White oak. Roble blanco.
Olive tree. Olivo.
Orange tree. Naranjo.

P

Palm. Palmera.

> **Corozo palm.** Corozo.
> **Date palm.** Datilero.
> **Fan palm.** Palmito, miraguano, palma llanera.
> **Peach palm.** Pejibaye.
> **Ponytail palm.** Pata de elefante.
> **Royal palm.** Palma caruta, palma de cerdos, de grana o de yagua.
> **Sago palm.** Palmero sagú.
> **Thatch palm.** Palma chit.

Palmetto. Palmito, palmera enana.

Palo blanco. Palo blanco.

Palo brea. Palo brea.

Palo verde. Palo verde.

Peach tree. Duraznero.

Pear tree. Peral.

Pecan tree. Pacana.

Pine. Pino.

> **Montezuma pine.** Ocote.
> **Norway pine.** Pino rojo.
> **Red pine.** Pino rojo.
> **Ponderosa pine.** Pino amarillo o ponderosa.
> **White pine.** Pino blanco.

Pine cone. Piña.

Pinyon tree. Piñon.

Plum tree. Ciruelo.

Poplar. Álamo.

> **Black poplar.** Álamo negro.
> **White poplar.** Álamo blanco.

Q

Quince tree. Membrillo, membrillero.

Redwood. Secoya, secuoya.

S
Sap. Savia.
Sassafras. Sasafrás.
Sequoia. Secoya, secuoya.
Sorrel tree. Oxidendro.
Spruce. Pícea.
    Blue spruce. Pícea azul.
    Red spruce. Pícea roja.
    White spruce. Pícea blanca.
Sweet gum. Liquidámber americano.
Sycamore. Sicóromo, sicoromo.

T
Teak. Teca.
Tree. Arbol.
Tree limb. Rama.
Twig. Ramita.
Tupelo. Tupelo.

W
Walnut. Nogal.
Willow. Sauce.

Y
Yew. Tejo.

GARDEN, GREENHOUSE & NURSERY
JARDÍN, INVERNADERO Y VIVERO

A
Abutment. Confin, linde.
Accent. Acento.
Acidity. Acidez.
   Acidic. Acídico, -a.
Adaptation. Adaptación.
   To adapt. Adaptarse.
Air conditioning. Aire condicionado.
Air duct. Tubo de ventilación.
Air flow. Flujo de aire.
Alien. Extranjero, -a; foreano, -a.
Alkaline. Alcalino, -a.
Alley. Callejón, callejuela.
Aluminum. Aluminio.
Ammonium. Amonio.
Application. Aplicación.
   To apply. Aplicar.
Aquatic. Acuático, -a.
Arbor. Pérgola, cenador.
Arcade. Galera.
Arch. Arco.
Artificial. Artificial.
Atrium. Atrio.
Ash. Ceniza.
Awning. Toldo, marquesina.

B
Balcony. Balcón.
Base. Base.
Bed. Macizo, parterre.
Bee. Abeja.

Bench. Banco, banca.
Berm. Berma.
Biodegradable. Biodegradable.
Bird feeder. Comedero de pájaros.
Birdhouse. Pajarera.
Bird nest. Nido.
Board. Tabla.
Boardwalk. Entablado.
Bog. Pantano, ciénaga, cenegal.
Boiler. Boiler, calentador, caldera, calefón.
Border. Parterre.
Bower. Emparrado, cenador.
Bushel. Bushel.
Builder. Constructor, -a.
Building. Estructura, inmueble.

C
Calcium. Calcio.
Canopy. Dosel.
Capacity. Capacidad.
Captan. Captan.
Carpenter. Carpintero, -a.
Cement slab. Losa.
Certified. Certificado, -a.
    To certify. Certificar.
Channel. Canal.
Chemical. Sustancia química, producto químico (n.);
químico, -a (adj.)
Chimney. Chimenea.
Circulation. Circulación.
Cistern. Cisterna.
Clay. Barro.
Clock. Reloj.
Code. Codigo.
Cold. Frío (n.), frío, -a (adj.)

Color. Color.

Column. Columna.

Compost. Compost.

    Soilless compost mixture. Mezcla de compost sin tierra.

Compound. Mezcla, compuesta.

Condensation. Condensación.

Condition. Condición.

Conservatory. Conservatorio.

Construction. Construcción.

    To construct. Construir.

Container. Contenedor.

Contour. Contorno, perfil.

Contractor. Contractor.

Control. Control.

Controller. Controlador.

Convection current. Corriente de convección.

Cool. Fresco, -a.

Course of bricks. Hilada de ladrillos.

Courtyard. Patio.

Crop. Cosecha, cultivo.

[To] Crop. Podar.

Cultivar. Variedad.

Cultivation. Cultivo.

    To cultivate. Cultivar.

Curb. Bordillo, encintado.

Cutting. Esqueje.

    To cut. Cortar.

D

Damp. Húmedo, -a.

Deficiency. Deficiencia.

Design. Diseño.

    To design. Diseñar.

[To] Dig. Excavar.

Dimension. Dimensión.
Direct. Directo, -a.
Diversity. Diversidad.
Division. División, separación.
Dome. Domo.
Dominant. Dominante.
Door. Puerta.
Downspout. Bajada de aguas.
Draft, draught. Corriente.
Drain. Drenaje, sumidero.
    Drainage. Desagüe.
    Drainpipe. Tubo de desagüe.
    To drain. Drenar, desaguar.
Drenched. Empapado.
    To drench. Empapar.
Driveway. Entrada, acceso.
Dry. Seco, -a.
    To dry. Secar.

E
Eave. Alero.
Ecosystem. Ecosistema.
Edge. Borde, parterre.
Electricity. Electricidad, luz.
    Electric. Eléctrico, -a.
    Electrical cable. Cable.
    Electrical outlet. Contacto.
    Electrician. Eléctrico, -a, electrecista.
Elevation. Elevación.
Enrichment. Fertilización.
Entrance. Entrada.
Environment. Entorno, ambiente.
    Environmental. Ambiental.
Equipment. Equipo.
Erosion. Erosión.

Excavation. Excavación.
   To excavate. Excavar.

F
Feeding. Alimentación.
Fence. Barda, cerca.
   Cyclone fence. Maya ciclónica.
   Picket fence. Cerca de madera.
Fertilizer. Fertilizante.
   Fertilization. Fertilización.
Field. Campo, sembrado, prado.
Fire. Fuego.
Firebreak. Cortafuego.
Fire pit. Pozo para hacer fuego.
Floor. Suelo.
Flooring. Solería, solado.
Floriferous. Floríféreo, -a.
Flower bed. Macizo.
Foliage. Follaje.
Footing. Base, pie, zapata.
Formaldehyde. Formaldehído.
Foundation. Cimientos.
Fountain. Fuente.
Frame. Marco.
Framework. Armazón.
Fuel. Combustible.
Fumigation. Fumigación.
   To fumigate. Fumigar.
Fungicide. Fungicida.
Furrow. Surco.

G
Garage. Garaje.
Garden. Jardín.
   Botanical garden. Jardín botánico.

Community garden. Jardín comunitario.
Gardener. Jardinero, -a.
Gate. Reja.
[To] Gather. Recoger.
Geodesic. Geodésico, -a.
Germination. Germinacion.
   To germinate. Germinar.
Glass. Vidrio.
Glazing. Vidriado, a cristalamiento.
[To] Grade. Aplanar, allanar.
Grading. Aplanamiento, nivelación.
Gradient. Ambulante, inclinación, pendiente.
Grafting. Injerto.
   To graft. Injertar.
Grass. Césped, prado.
Grassland. Pradera.
Grate. Enrejado, reja.
Greenhouse. Inverdadero.
Grille. Enrejado, reja.
Grit. Arenilla, gravilla.
Ground. Tierra, terreno.
Groundcover. Cobertura de suelo.
[To] Grow. Cultivar.
Growing season. Temporada o época de cultivo.
Gutter. Canaleta, canalón.

H
Hard. Duro, -a.
Hardy. Resistente, robusto, -a.
Harvest. Cosecha.
   To harvest. Cosechar.
Healthy. Sano, -a.
Heat. Calor.
   Heat loss. Pérdida de calor.
Hedge. Seto.

Herbicide. Herbicida.
Hibernation. Hibernación.
   To hibernate. Hibernar.
Hollow. Vacio, -a.
[To] Hone. Afilar.
Hosepipe. Manguera, manga.
Hot. Caliente.
House. Casa.
Humidity. Humidad.
Humus. Humus.
Hydroponics. Hidroponía.
   Hydroponic. Hidropónico, -a
Illumination. Iluminación.

I

Insoluble. Insoluble.

L

Land. Tierra, terreno.
Landscaping. Paisajismo.
Lath. Listón.
Lawn. Césped, prado.
Leak. Fuga, escape, gotera.
Lean-to. Cobertizo.
Level. A nivel; nivelado, -a.
Light. Luz.
Lighting. Alumbrado, iluminación
Loam. Loam.
Loose. Suelto, -a.
Lot. Lote.
Louvre. Persiana.
Lumen. Lumen.

M

Magnesium. Magnesio.

Maintenance. Mantamiento.
Manganese. Manganeso.
Manure. Estiércol.
Marsh. Ciénaga, pantano.
Masonry. Albañilería.
  Mason. Albañil, -a.
Mature. Maduro, -a.
To mature. Madurar.
Meadow. Pradera, prado.
Measurement. Medida.
Mechanism. Mecanismo.
Mist. Rocio.
  To mist. Rociar.
Mix, mixture. Mezcla.
  To mix. Mezclar.
Monitor. Monitor.
Monoculture. Monocultura.
Moss. Turba.
[To] Mow. Cortar.
Mulch. Mantillo, abono.

N
Nature. Naturaleza.
  Natural. Natural.
New. Nuevo, -a.
Nitrate. Nitrato.
  Ammonium nitrate. Nitrato de amonio.
  Potassium nitrate. Nitrato de potasio.
Nitrogen. Nitrógeno.
Nursery. Vivero.
Nutrient. Nutriente.
  Nutrition. Nutrición

O
Old. Viejo, -a; maduro, -a.

Organic. Orgánico, -a.
Organophosphorus. Organofósoro, -a.
Ornamental. Decorativo, -a, ornamental.

P
[To] Oxygenate. Oxigenar.
Pale (fence post). Reja.
Panel. Panel, tablero.
Part. Parte.
Path. Sendero.
Pattern. Patrón.
Paving. Pavimentación.
Pedestal. Pedestal.
Pergola. Pérgola.
Perspective. Perspectiva.
Pesticide. Pesticida.
pH. pH.
Phosphate. Fosfato.
Phosphorus. Fósforo.
Photoperiodic. Fotoperiódico, -a.
Photosynthesis. Fotosintesis.
[To] Pick. Coger.
Pipe. Tubo.
Pitch of a roof. Declive, pendiente.
Planning. Planeación.
    Plans. Planes, dibujos.
    To plan. Planear.
[To] Plant. Plantar, sembrar.
    Planting. Siembra.
Plant community. Comunidad de plantas.
Plastic. Plástico (n.), plástico, -a (adj.).
Platform. Plataforma.
Plaza. Plaza.
Plumbing. Plomería.
Pollination. Polinación.

To pollinate. Polinar.

Pond, pool. Estanque.

Porch, pórtico. Pórtico.

Portability. Portabilidad.

Position. Posición.

Pot. Maceta.

    Clay plot. Maceta de barro.

[To] Pot. Plantar en maceta.

Potash. Potasa.

Potassium. Potasio.

Potting mix. Mezcla para macetas.

Preserve (location). Preserva.

Privacy. Privacidad, privación.

Project. Proyecto.

Propagation. Propagación.

    Propagator. Propagador.

Property. Propiadad.

Pruning. Poda.

    To prune. Podar.

Pulverized. Pulverizado, -a

Putty. Mastique, masilla.

R

Raised. Elevado, -a.

Rammed earth. Tierra apisonada.

Ramp. Rampa.

Raw materials. Materia prima o bruta.

Reflector. Reflectador.

Repair, repairing. Reparación.

    To repair. Reparar.

[To] Require. Requerir.

Respiration. Resperación.

Riparian. Ribereño, -a.

Ripe. Maduro, -a.

Rivulet. Riachuelo.

Road. Camino, calle.
Roof. Techo, tejado.
Rooftop terrace. Azotea, techo.
Rot. Pudrimiento.
    Rotted. Pudrido, -a.
    To rot. Pudrirse.
Row. Hilera.

S
Savanna. Sabana.
Season. Estación, temporada.
Section. Sección.
Security. Seguridad.
Seed. Semilla.
Seepage in. Fuga.
    Seepage out. Filtración.
Sensor. Sensor.
Shade. Sombra.
    Shady. Sombreado, -a.
[To] Sharpen. Afilar.
Shed. Cobertizo, depósito.
Shelf. Estante.
Sheltered. Protegido, -a; resguardado, -a.
Site. Sitio.
    Site orientation. Orentación de sitio.
    Site-specific. In situ.
Size. Tamaño, medida.
Skylight. Tragaluz.
Slat. Listón.
Smell, odor. Olor.
Smooth. Liso, -a.
Soft. Suelto, -a; suave.
Soil. Tierra.
Solar. Solar.
    Solar energy. Energía solar.

Solar radiation. Radiación solar.
Solid. Sólido, -a.
[To] Sow. Sembrar.
Space. Espacio.
Species. Especie.
Spray. Rociada.
    To spray. Rociar.
Stair. Escalón.
Standardization. Estandardización.
Steam. Vapor.
Step. Escalón.
Sterilization. Estirilización.
Stonework. Construcción de piedra.
    Stonemason. Cantero, -a.
Storage shed. Cobertizo, depósito.
Storeroom. Bodega.
Straw. Paja.
Structure. Estructura.
Stunted. Retrasado, -a.
Street. Calle.
Succession. Sucesión.
Sulphate. Sulfato.
Sun. Sol.
    Sunlight. Luz solar.
    Sunny. Soleado, -a.
Sunken. A nivel más bajo, al ras de suelo; hundido, -a.
Supplementary light. Luz suplementaria.
Surface. Superficie.
Swamp. Pantano, ciénaga.
System. Sistema.

T
[To] tamp. Pisar.
    Tamped earth. Tierra apisonada.
Temperate. Temporado, -a.

Temperature. Temperatura.
Terrace. Terraza, azotea.
Terrain. Terreno.
Thermometer. Termómetro.
Thermostat. Termostato.
Thickness. Espesor.
[To] Till. Arar, cultivar, labrar.
Timber. Madera.
Tolerant. Tolerante.
Topiary. Topiaria.
Topography. Topografía.
Toxicity. Toxicidad.
Translucent. Trasluciente.
Transparent. Transparente.
Transpiration. Transpiración.
Treatment. Tratamiento.
Trellis. Enrejado.
[To] Trickle. Escurrirse.
Tropical. Tropical.

U
Underground. Subterráneo, -a.

V
Ventilation. Ventilación.
    Vent. Conducto o rejilla de ventilación.
    Ventilated. Ventilado, -a.
Ventilator. Ventilador.
Veranda. Veranda, galera.
Vermiculite. Vermiculita.
View. Vista.
Voltage. Voltaje.

W
Wall. Muro, pared.

Partition wall. Pared divisoria.

Retaining wall. Muro de retén.

Water. Agua.

To wáter. Regar.

Watering. Riego.

Water vapor. Vapor de agua.

Waterproof. Impermeable.

Water table. Nivel hidrostático, capa de agua.

Wet. Mojado, -a.

Wetland. Pantano.

Wildlife. Fauna, vida salvaje.

Windbreak. Cortavientos, rompevientos.

Window. Ventana.

Windowbox. Maceta para barandilla, maceta de balcón.

Woodland (n.) Bosque.

Woodland (adj.) Del bosque.

Work crew. Equipo.

Workshop. Taller.

Y
Yard. Patio.

Z
Zone. Zona.

TOOLS, MATERIALS AND HARDWARE
HERRAMIENTAS, MATERIALES Y FERRETERÍA

A
Aerator. Aireador.
Aggregate. Agregado.
Attachment. Accesorio.
Auger. Barreno, sonda.
Ax, axe. Hacha.

B
Backhoe. Retroexcavadora.
Bag. Bolsa.
Ball. Bola.
Bar. Barreta.
Basket. Canasta.
Bin. Contenador.
Bit. Broca.
Block. Bloque.
Board. Tabla.
Bobcat. Mini-cargador.
Box. Caja.
Bracket. Mensula.
Brick. Ladrillo.
Broom. Escoba.
Brush. Cepillo.
Brush cutter. Desbrozadora, cortadora de malezas.
Bucket. Cubeta.
Building materials. Materiales de construcción.
Bulldozer. Bulldozer.
Burlap. Arpillera, yute.

C
Cable. Cable.
Carpenter's square. Escuadra.

Cement. Cemento.
Chain. Cadena.
Cinder block. Tabicón, tabique.
Clamp. Prensa, torno de mano, brida.
Cleaner. Limpiador.
Cobblestone. Adoquín.
Compressor. Compresora.
Concrete. Concreto.
Connector. Conector, conectador, unión.
Cord. Cordel, cuerda, lazo.
Corrugated metal. Metal ondulado, lámina.
Coupling. Acople, cople, conexión.
Crane. Grúa.

D
Dirt, earth. Tierra.
Drill bit. Broca
Dump truck. Volquete.

E
Ear muffs. Orejeras.
Edger. Bordeadora, orilladora.
Excavator. Excavadora.
Extension. Extensión.
Extender. Extensor.
Faucet. Llave.

F
Feeder. Alimentador.
Fence post. Poste.
   Fence post digger. Cavador.
Fibreglass. Fibra de vidrio.
Filter. Filtro, coladera.
Front-end loader. Cargador frontal.

G

Garbage can. Bote de basura.
Generator. Generador.
Gloves. Guantes.
Grader. Montoniveladora.
Guide. Guía.

H

Hammer. Martillo.
    Sledge hammer. Marro, almádana, almádena.
Handle. Mango.
Hanger. Gancho.
Hardware. Ferretería.
Heater. Calefactor.
    Heating. Calefacción.
    Heat exchanger. Intercambiador de calor.
Hessian. Arpillera.
Hinge. Bisagra.
Hoe. Azada.
Hook. Gancho.
Hose. Mangera.
    Flexible hose. Mangera flexible.
Humidifier. Humedecedor.
Hydraulic shovel. Pala hidráulica.

I

Insulation. Aislamiento.
    Insulated. Aislado, -a.
    To insulate. Aislar.
Iron. Hierro.
Cast iron. Hierro colado.
    Wrought iron. Hierro forjado o labrado.

J

Jet. Merchero, sutidor.

Joist. Viga, vigueta.

K
Key. Llave.
Knee pad. Rodillera.
Knife. Cuchillo, navaja.
    Utility knife. Navaja, retracil.

L
Ladder. Escala.
Lath. Listón, enlistonado.
Leaf blower. Sopladora.
Light bulb. Foco, bombillo.
Lime. Cal.
Line. Hilo.
Liner. Revestimiento, interior, forro.
Liquid. Líquido (n.); líquido, -a (adj.).
Load. Cargo, peso.

M
Machete. Machete.
Machine. Máquina.
Mallet. Mazo.
Maul. Marro.
Mirror. Espejo.
Mixer. Mezcladora.
    Cement mixer. Revolvadora.
Motor. Motor.

N
Nail. Clavo.
Net. Red.
Nozzle. Chiflón.
Nut. Tuerca.

P

Paint. Pintura.

  Paint thinner. Thinner.

Paver. Pavimentadora.

Paving stone. Adoquín, losa.

Peat, peat moss. Turba.

  Peat pot. Maceta de turba.

Peg. Clavija.

Pencil. Lápiz.

Perlite. Perlita.

Pick, pickax. Pico.

Pickaxe. Pico, zapapico.

Pincers. Pinzas, tenazas.

Pipe. Tubo.

Pitchfork. Bieldo.

Plank. Tablón.

Planter. Maceta, tiesto, macetero.

Planter (machine). Sembradora.

Plastic. Plástico (n.); plástico, -a (adj.).

Plastic sheeting. Rollo de hule o plástico.

Pliers. Pinzas, alicates.

  Needle-nose pliers. Pinza de punta.

Plug. Tapa, plug.

Plywood. Triplay, madera contrachapada o terciada, triplex.

Polythene. Polietileno.

Post hole digger. Cavador.

Pot. Maceta.

Power supply box. Centro o caja de cargo.

Pressure. Presión.

  High pressure. Alta presión o alto volumen.

  Low pressure. Baja presión o bajo volumen.

Pressurized. Presurizado, a.

  To pressurize. Presurizar.

Pruning shears. Podadera, tijera de podar.

Pump. Bomba.
>**Submergible pump.** Bomba sumergible.
>**Water pump.** Bomba de agua.
>**To pump.** Bombear, sacar con una bomba.

PVC. PVC.
Pry bar. Barreta, palanca.
Pulley. Pulea.
PVC. PVC.

R

Rag. Trapo.
Rake. Rastrillo.
Rammed earth. Tierra apisonada.
>**Rammer.** Pisón.

Replacement. Repuesto.
Rod. Barra.
Roll. Rollo.
Roller. Roller.
Roof tile. Teja.
Rope. Reata, cuerda, amarra.
Ruler. Metro.

S

Sand. Arena.
Saw. Sierra.
>**Bow saw.** Sierra arco.
>**Chainsaw.** Motosierra.
>**Hack saw.** Sierra arco, sierra de metals.
>**Handsaw.** Sierra de mano, serrote, serucho.
>**Hole saw.** Cortacirculos.
>**Rip saw.** Sierra de abrazadera.
>**Saw blade.** Hoja de sierra.

[To] saw. Serrar, aserrar.
Scissors. Tijeras.
Screen (wire mesh). Mosquitero, maya.

Screen window. Mosquitero.

Screen (partition). Biombo.

Screw. Tornillo.

Screwdriver. Desarmador, destornillador.

> **Flathead screwdriver.** Desarmador estandard.

> **Phillips screwcdriver.** Desarmador Phillips o de cruz.

Set of. Juego de (e.g. 'set of wrenches,' juego de llaves).

Shank. Mango.

Sharpener. Afilador, amolador

Sheers. Cizalla.

Sheet metal. Lámina.

Shingle. Tablilla.

Shovel. Pala.

Sink. Lavabo, fregadora.

Sower. Desparramador, sembrador.

Spacer. Espaciador.

Sprayer. Rociador.

Spreader. Extendadora.

Sprinkler. Aspersor.

Stake. Estaca.

Syringe. Jeringa.

System. Sistema.

T

Table. Mesa.

Tank. Tanque.

> **Storage tank.** Tanque de almacenamiento.

> **Water tank.** Aljibe, tanque de agua, tinaco.

Tape. Cinta.

> **Electrical tape.** Cinta eléctrica.

> **Masking tape.** Cinta masking.

> **Teflon tape.** Cinta teflón.

Tarp. Lona.

Terra cotta. Terracota.
Thatch. Paja.
   Thatched roof. Techo de paja.
Tile. Azulejo.
Timer. Temporizador.
Tongs. Alicates, tenazas.
Tool. Herramienta.
   Tool box. Caja de herramientas.
Tractor. Tractor.
Trap. Trampa.
Trash can. Bote o contenedor de basura.
Tray. Charola.
Trimmer. Debastadora.
Truck. Camión.
Tub. Cuba, cubo.
Tube. Tubo.
   Tubing. Tubería.
Twine. Cordel, cuerda, bramante.

V
Valve. Válvula.
   Globe or spherical valve. Válvula esférica.
   Safety valve. Válvula de seguridad.
Ventilator. Ventilador.
Vibrator. Vibrador.
Vinyl. Vinilo.

W
Watering can. Regadora.
Water meter. Contador de agua.
Weed cutter or whacker. Cortadora de malezas, desbrozadora.
Wheel. Llanta, rueda.
Wheelbarrow. Carretilla.
Whetstone. Amolador.

Winch. Malacate.

Wire. Alambre, cable.

    Barbed wire. Alambre de púas.

Wire cutter. Cizalla, cortaalambres, tenazas de corte.

Wood. Madera.

Work bench. Banca de trabajo.

Wrench. Llave.

    Adjustable wrench. Llave adjustable.

    Crescent wrench. Llave fostada.

    Jaw (of a wrench). Muela.

    Socket wrench. Llave de dado, matraca.

TYPES OF STONE
TIPOS DE PIEDRA

B
Basalt. Basalto.

C
Chert. Calcedonia, pedernal.

F
Firestone. Pirita.
Flagstone. Enlosado.

G
Gabbro. Gabro.
Gneiss. Gneis.
Granite. Granito.
Gravel. Grava, gravilla.

L
Limestone. Caliza.

M
Marble. Mármol.

O
Onyx. Ónix, ónice.

P
Pebble. Guijarro, piedrecita, piedrita.
Pumice. Piedra pómez.

Q
Quarry. Cantera.
Quartz. Cuartzo.

R
Rock. Piedra, roca

S
Sandstone. Aspersón.
Schist. Esquito.
Slate. Pizzara.
Stone. Pidra.

T
Travertine. Mármol travertino.
Tufa. Toba calcárea.

COLORS/COLORES

A
Alabaster. Alabastrino.
Amber. Ámbar.
Aquamarine. Aguamarina, azul verdoso.
Auburn. Castaño rojizo.

B
Beige. Beige, beis.
Black. Negro, -a.
Blue. Azul.
    Midnight blue. Azul de medianoche, azul oscuro.
    Powder blue. Azul cielo o claro, celeste perlado.
    Sky blue. Azul celeste.
    Steel blue. Azul metálico.
Brown. Café, marrón, castaño.
Buff. Beige, beis.
Burgundy. Borgoña, bermellón.

C
Carmine. Carmín.
Cerulean. Cerúleo.
Color. Color.
Copper. Cobrizo, -a.
Coral. Coral.
Cream. Color crema.
Crimson. Carmesí.

D
Drab. Marrón oliva.
Dun. Pardo.

E
Ebony. Ébono.

G

Garnet. Granate, burdeos.
Gold. Dorado, -a.
Gray, grey. Gris.
    Dove gray. Gris paloma.
    Silver gray. Plateado, gris plateado.
    Slate gray. Gris oscuro, gris pizarra.
Green. Verde.
    Blue green. Aguamarina, azul verdoso, verde azul, verdiazul.
    Emerald green. Verde esmeralda.
    Forrest green. Verde bosque.
    Hunter green. Verde oscuro.
    Jade Green. Verde turquesa.
    Kelly green. Verde brillante.
    Moss green. Verde musgo.

I

Ivory. Marfil.

L

Lavender. Lavanda, lila.

M

Magenta. Purpúreo rojizo.
Mauve. Malva.

O

Ochre. Ocre.
Orange. Anaranjado, -a; de color naranjo.
Oxblood. Guinda, rojo oscuro.

P

Pink. Rosa.
Purple. Purpúreo, violeta.

R

Red. Rojo, -a.
Russet. Castaño rojizo, marrón rojizo.
Rust. Teja.

S

Salmon. Color salmón.
Scarlet. Escarlata.
Shade. Tono, matiz.
Sienna. Siena.
Silver. Platiado, -a.
Striped. Rayado, -a.

T

Taupe. Gris topo, marrón topo.
Translucent. Trasluciente.
Turquoise. Turquesa.

U

Ultramarine. Azul de ultramar, ultramarino, ultramaro.
Umber. Marrón oscuro, ocre.

V

Variegation. Variegación.
   Variegated. Multicolor, variado.
Verdigris. Verdín, cardenillo.
Vermilion. Bermellón.
Violet. Violet.
Viridian. Verde esmeralda.

W

White. Blanco, -a.

Y

Yellow. Amarillo, -a.

SEASONS, MONTHS, THE DAY, DIRECTIONS

ESTACIONES DEL AÑO, MESES, EL DÍA, DIRECCIONES

Seasons. Estaciones del año

Spring. Primavera.
Summer. Verano.
Autumn, fall. Otoño.
Winter. Invierno.

Months. Meses.

January. Enero.
February. Febrero.
March. Marzo
April. Abril.
May. Mayo.
June. Junio.
July. Julio.
August. Agosto.
September. Septiembre.
October. Octubre.
November. Noviembre.
December. Diciembre.

The day. El día.

Dawn. Amanecer, alba.
Morning. Mañana.
Midday, noon. Mediodía.
Aftenoon. Tarde.
Late afternoon. Atardecer.
Evening. Por la tarde.
Night. Noche.

Directions. Direcciones.

East. Este (n. y adj.), hacia el este, al este (in the direction of).

North. Norte (n.), nor (adj.), hacia el norte, al norte (in the direction of).

Northeast. Noreste.

Northwest. Noroeste.

South. Sur (n. y adj.), hacia el sur, al sur (in the direction of).

Southeast. Sureste.

Southwest. Suroeste.

West. Oeste (n.), oeste, occidental (adj.), hacia el oeste, al oeste (in the direction of).

MEASUREMENTS AND DIMENSIONS

MEDIDAS Y DIMENSIONES

A
Acre. Acre.
Angle. Ángulo.
    Angular. Ángular.
Area. Área, superficie.
Average. Medio, promedio.

C
Calculation. Cálculo.
Capacity. Capacidad.
Celsius. Celsio.
Center. Centro.
Centimeter. Centímetro.
Circle. Círculo.
    Circular. Circular.
Circumference. Circunferencia.
Circumscribe. Circunscribir.
Cubic. Cúbico, -a.

D
Decimal. Decimal.
Degree. Grado.
Depth. Profundidad.
    Deep. Profundo, -a.
Diameter. Diametro.
Dimension. Dimensión.
Distance. Distancía.
Dozen. Docena.

E
Equidistant. Equidistante.

Estimation. Estimación.
>**To estimate.** Estimar.
External, outside. Externo, -a.

F
Fahreinheit. Fahreinheit.
Foot. Pie.
>**Square foot.** Pie cuadrado.
>**Cubic foot.** Pie cúbito.

G
Gallon. Galón.
Gradient. Ambulante, inclinación, pendiente.
Graph. Gráfica.

H
Hectare. Hectárea.
Heigth. Altura.
>**High.** Alto, -a.
Horizontal. Horizontal.

I
Inch. Pulgada.
Inside, internal. Interno, -a.

K
Kilogram. Kilo, kilogramo.

L
Lateral. Lateral.
Left. Izquierdo, -a.
Length. Largura.
>**Long.** Largo, -a.
Limit. Límite.
Linear. Lineal.
Liter. Litro.

M
Maximum. Máximo.
Measurement. Medida.
    To measure. Medir.
Meter. Metro.
    Square meter. Metro cuadrado.
    Cubic meter. Metro cúbito.
Millimeter. Milímetro.
Minimum. Mínimo.

N
Number. Número.

O
Ounce. Onza.
Oval. Ovalado, -a.

P
Percent. Por ciento, Porcentaje.
Perspective. Perspectiva.
Pound. Libra.

Q
Quantity. Cantidad.

R
Rectangle. Rectángulo.
    Rectangular. Rectangular.
Right. Derecho, -a.

S
Scale (i.e. dimensional). Escala.
Segment. Segmento.
Side. Lado.
Solid. Sólido.
Span. Distancia.

Speed. Velocidad.
Square. Cuadra (n.); cuadrado, -a (adj.).
Straight. Derecho, -a.
Surface. Superficie.
Symmetrical. Simétrico, -a.

T

Temperature. Temperatura.
Thickness. Espesor, grueso.
Ton. Tonelada.
    Metric ton. Tonelada métrico.
Triangular. Triangular.

V

Vertical. Vertical, plumb.

W

Weight. Peso, pesa.
Width. Anchura.
    Wide. Ancho, -a.

Y

Yard. Yarda.
    Square yard. Yarda cuadrada.
    Cubic yard. Yarda cúbita.

NUMBERS/NÚMEROS

One, 1. Uno.
Two, 2. Dos.
Three, 3. Tres.
Four, 4. Cuatro.
Five, 5. Cinco.
Six, 6. Seis.
Seven, 7. Siete.
Eight, 8. Ocho.
Nine, 9. Nueve.
Ten, 10. Diez.
Eleven, 11. Once.
Twelve, 12. Doce.
Thirteen, 13. Trece.
Fourteen, 14. Catorce.
Fifteen, 15. Quince.
Sixteen, 16. Dieciseis.
Seventeen, 17. Diecisiete.
Eighteen, 18. Dieciocho.
Nineteen, 19. Diecinueve.
Twenty, 20. Veinte.
Thirty, 30. Treinta.
Forty, 40. Cuarenta.
Fifty, 50. Cincuenta.
Sixty, 60. Sesenta.
Seventy, 70. Setenta.
Eighty, 80. Ochenta.
Ninety, 90. Noventa.
Hundred, 100. Cien, ciento.
Thousand, 1000. Mil.

Fractions/Fracciones

Half, 1/2. Medio, -a.
Third, 1/3. Tercero, -a.

Quarter, 1/4. Cuarto, -a.
Fifth, 1/5. Quinto, -a.
Sixth, 1/6. Sexto, -a.
Seventh, 1/7. Séptimo, -a.
Eighth, 1/8. Octavo, -a.
Ninth. 1/9. Noveno, -a
Tenth, 1/10. Decimo, -a.
Sixteenth, 1/16. Décimosexto, -a.
Thirty-second, 1/32. Trigésimo-segundo, -a.
Sixty-fourth, 1/64. Sexagésimo-cuarto, -a.

GARDEN PESTS AND DISEASES
PESTES, PLAGAS Y ENFERMIDADES

A
Ant. Hormiga.
    Cutter ant. Hormiga cortadora.
Aphid. Áfido, pulgón.
Armyworm. Cogollero de maíz, gardama, gusano cogollero.

B
Beetle. Escarabajo.
Blight. Plaga.
Borer. Broma.

C
Canker. Cancro.
Capsid. Chinche.
Caterpillar. Aruga.
Chlorosis. Clorosis.
Cutworm. Cortadora, gusano cortador.

D
Defoliation. Defoliación.
Discoloration. Decoloración.
Disease. Enfermidad.
    Diseased. Enfermo, -a.

E
Earworm. Esrosquilla.
Egg. Huevo.

F
Fly. Mosca.
Frost. Escarcha.

Fungus. Moho, micosis.
    Fungal. Micótico, -a; fúngico, -a.
Fusarium wilt. Fusarium marchita.

G
Gall. Agalla.
Gopher. Taltuza, tuza.
Grasshopper. Chapulín, saltamontes.
Grub worm. Gallina ciega.

H
Halo. Halo.
Hornworm. Gusano córneo.

I
Infected. Infectado, -a.

L
Larvae. Larva.
Leafhopper. Chicharra.
Lesion. Lesión.
Locust. Chapulín, langosta.

M
Maggot. Larva, cresa.
Mildew. Mildew, mildiu, roya.
Millepede. Milpiés.
Mite. Ácaro.
Mold. Hongo.
Mole. Topo.
Moribund. Moribundo, -a.
Mosaic virus. Virus mosaico.
Moth larvae. Larva de polilla.
Mottling. Moteado.
Mouse. Ratón.

N
Nematode. Nematodo.

P
Pest. Peste, plaga.

R
Rat. Rata.
Rust. Roya.

S
Scorch. Escaladura.
Shipworm. Broma.
Slater. Cochinilla.
Slime. Baba.
Slug. Babosa.
Smut. Tizón.
Snail. Caracol.
Spider. Araña.
    Spiderweb. Telaraña.
Spot. Mancha.
Springtail. Colémbolo.

T
Thrips. Arañuela.

V
Verticillium wilt. Verticillium marchita.
Virus. Virus.

W
Weed. Mala hierba, maleza.
Weevil. Gorgojo.
    Boll weevil. Gorgojo de algodón, picudo.
    Root weevil. Gorgojo de las raices.
Whitefly. Mosca blanca, mosquita blanca.

Wilt. Marchita.

    To wilt. Marchitarse.

Wireworm. Gusano de elatérido.

Woodlice. Cochinilla.

Worm. Gusano.

ESPAÑOL/INGLÉS

SPANISH/ENGLISH

FLORES, PLANTAS, ARBUSTOS
FLOWERS, PLANTS, SHRUBS

A

Acebo. Holly.
Acedera. Dock.
Aciano. Bluebonnet, bluet, cornflower.
Adelfa. Dogbane, oleander.
Adianto. Maidenhair fern.
Aguileña. Columbine.
Ajuga. Ajuga.
Alazor. Safflower.
Alcatraz. Calla lily.
Alegría. Sunpatiens.
Alegría de la casa. Impatiens, patient Lucy.
Algarroba. Vetch.
Algodón. Cotton.
Algondoncillo. Milkweed.
Alheña, aligustre. Privet.
Aliso. Allysum.
Altramuz. White lupin.
Altramuz azul. Bluebonnet.
Alverjilla. Sweet pea.
Amapola. Poppy.
Amarilis. Amaryllis.
Ambrosia. Ambrosia.
Anémona. Anemone.
Anual. Annual.
Antirrino. Antirrhinum.
Aquilea. Yarrow.
Arbusto. Bush, shrub.
Aro. Arum.
Aronia. Chokeberry.
Arrayán. Myrtle.

Asclepia. Asclepia.
Áster. Aster.
Atanasia. Tansy.
Ave de paraíso. Bird of Paradise.
Avellano de bruja. Witch hazel.
Azafrán. Crocus.
Azalea. Azalea, rhododendrun.
Azucena. Lily, lirio.

B
Bambú. Bamboo.
Begonia. Begonia.
Bergenia. Elephant's ears.
Boca de león o dragón. Antirrhinum, snapdragon.
Botón de oro. Buttercup.
Bráctea. Bráct.
Brezo. Heather.
Brizna. Grass blade.
Bromelia. Bromeliad.
Brotar. To bud.
Brote. Shoot, sprout.
Buganvilla. Bougainvillea.
Bulbo. Bulb, corm.

C
Cactus, cacto. Cactus.
Calatea. Calathea.
Calceolaria. Calceolaria.
Caléndula. Marigold.
Cáliz. Calyx.
Camelia. Camellia.
Campanilla, campánula. Bluebell, harebell, morning glory.
Campanilla de invierno. Snowdrop.
Campanilla verdezuela. Bellflower.

Campanita. Morning glory.
Caña. Cane.
Capuchina. Nasturtium.
Capullo. Bud.
Cardo. Cardoon, thistle.
Carrizo. Bamboo-like reed.
Cártamo. Safflower.
Casia. Cassia.
Castaño de Indias. Buckeye.
Celtis. Hackberry.
Cenizo, ceniza. Cenizo.
Centeno. Rye.
Césped. Sod.
Césped ornamental. Mondo grass.
Chaparral. Chaparral.
Ciclamen, ciclamino. Cyclamen.
Cicuta. Hemlock.
Cineraria. Cineraria.
Clavel. Carnation, dianthus.
Clavelina. Dianthus.
Clemátide. Clematis.
Col de mofeta occidental o amarillo (Lysichiton americanus). Skunk cabbage.
Col de mofeta oriental, col de los prados o pantanos (Symplocartus foetidus). Skunk cabbage.
Cóleo. Coleus.
Conejito. Snapdragon.
Consuelda. Larkspur.
Copa de rey. Columbine.
Corazón sagrante. Dicentra, lyreflower.
Cornejo. Cornel.
Corona de flores. Wreath.
Creosote Bush. Creosota.
Cresta de gallo. Cockscomb, coxcomb.
Crisantemo. Chrysanthemum, mum.

Croco. Crocus.
Croton. Croton.
Corona. Crown.
Culantrillo. Maidenhair fern.
Culmo. Culm.
Cultivar. Cultivar, variety.

D
Dalia. Dahlia.
Daphne. Daphne.
Daze azul. Evolvulus.
Dedalera. Foxglove.
Delfinio. Delphinium.
Dentabrón. Male fern.
Diente de león. Dandelion.
Digital. Foxglove.
Dionaea atrapamoscas, dionaea muscipula. Venus
flytrap.
Dracaena. Dracaena.

E
Enano, -a. Dwarf.
Enea. Bulrush.
Enredadera. Climber, creeper, vine.
Epifita. Epiphyte.
    Epifítico, -a. Epiphytic.
Equinácea. Coneflower.
Ericaceo, -a. Ericaceous.
Escoba de bruja. Witch hazel.
Esfagno. Sphagnum moss.
Espadaña. Bulrush, cattail.
Espata. Spathe.
Espora. Spore.
Espuela de caballero. Larkspur.
Estolón. Runner.

Estramonio. Jimsomweed.
Estrella de Belén. Star of Bethlehem.
Etusa. Hemlock.
Euforbia, euforbio. Spurge.
Evólvulo. Evolvulus.
Exótico, -a. Exotic.

F
Falso jazmín. Potato vine.
Follaje. Fan.
Ficus. Ficus.
Flor, floración. Flower, bloom.
    Florecer. To bloom.
Flor de Pascua. Poinsettia.
Flor silvestre. Wildflower.
Flox. Phlox.
Folíolo, foliolo. Leaflet.
Forbe. Forb, phorb.
Fresia. Freesia.
Fronda. Frond.
Frondosidad. Leafiness.
Fuchsia. Fucsia.

G
Gardenia. Gardenia.
Genciana. Gentian.
Génio. Genus.
Geranio. Geranium.
Girasol. Sunflower.
Gisófila. Gypsophila.
Gladiola, -o. Gladiola.
Glicinia. Wisteria.
Guirnalda. Garland, wreath.
Guisante de olor. Sweet pea.

H

Hábitat. Habitat.
Helecho. Fern.
    Helecho de haya largo o estrecho. Beech fern.
    Helecho macho. Male fern.
    Helecho real. Royal fern.
Heliotropo. Heliotrope.
Herboso, -a. Grassy.
Herbáceo, -a. Herbaceous.
Hibisco. Hibiscus.
Híbrido. Hybrid.
Hiedra. Ivy.
Hiedra venenosa. Poison ivy.
Hierba cana. Ragwort.
Hierba de Santa María o lombriguera. Tansy.
Hierba doncella. Periwinkle.
Hippeastrum. Hippeastrum.
Hoja. Leaf.
Hoja de helecho o palmera. Frond.
Hortensia. Hydrangea.
Hosta. Hosta.

I

Indigo. Indigo.
Intrusivo, -a. Intrusive.
Iris. Iris.

J

Jacinto. Hyacinth.
    Jacinto silvestre. Bluebell, wild or wood hyacinth.
Jaro. Arum.
Jazmín. Jasmine, jessamine.
Jazmín solano. Potato vine.
Jengibre. Ginger.
Juncia, junco. Marsh grass, reed, rush, sedge.

L

Lagerstromia. Crape or crepe myrtle.

Lantana. Lantana.

Lapa. Burr plant.

Laurel de San Antonio. Fireweed.

Lenteja de agua. Duckweed.

Leñoso, -a. Woody (i.e. thick, tough).

Liana. Liana.

Ligustro. Privet.

Lila. Lilac.

Lilo. Lilac.

Lino. Flax.

Linaza. Linseed.

Liquen. Lichen.

Lirio. Lily.

> **Lirio acuático.** Waterlily.

> **Lirio atigrado.** Tiger Lily.

Lobelia. Lobelia.

Lonchite. Hard fern.

Lupininus. Lupin.

M

Madreselva. Honeysuckle.

> **Madreselva de trompeta o de coral.** Trumpet honeysuckle.

Majuelo. Quickthorn.

Maíz de ardilla. Dicentra.

Mala hierba, maleza. Weed.

Malva arbórea, real o rósea; malvarrosa. Hollyhock.

Margarita. Daisy, marguerite.

Mata, matorral. Bush.

Mata de hierba. Tussock.

Matorral. Shrub, thicket.

Menta de lobo. Bugleweed.

Meristemo. Meristem.

Mesquite. Mesquite.
Milenrama. Yarrow.
Mimosa. Mimosa.
Mirabel, mirasol. Sunflower.
Mirto. Myrtle.
    Mirto de Brabantem o mirto de turbertra. Bog myrtle.
Moco de pavo. Cock's comb, cockscomb, coxcomb.
Morera. Mulberry.
Musgo. Moss.

N
Nenúfar. Waterlily.
Narciso. Daffodil, narcissus.
Nardo. Spikenard.
Nativo, -a. Native.
Nomeolvides. Forget-me-not.
Nochebuena. Poinsettia.
No intrusivo, -a. Nonintrusive.
Nube de novia. Gypsophila.

O
Oca. Wood sorrel.
Orquídea. Orchid.
Ortiga. Nettle.

P
Palmilla. Soaptree.
Panícula, panoja. Panicle.
Parra. Vine.
Pasionaria. Passion flower.
Pasto. Grass.
    Pastoso, -a. Grassy.
Pasto pennisetum. Fountain grass.
Pasto varilla. Switchgrass.
Pedúnculo. Pedicel.
Pelargonio. Pelargonium. 81

Penca. Fleshy leaf or rib of an agave.
Pensamiento. Pansy.
Peonía. Peony.
Peperomia. Peperomia.
Perenne. Perennial.
Pétalo. Petal.
Peciolo. Petiole.
Petunia. Petunia.
Pimienta. Peperomia.
Planta. Plant.
Planta corredora o rodadora. Tumbleweed.
Planta de interior. Houseplant.
Planta de semillero, plantón. Seedling.
Planta salvaje. Wilding.
Planta trepadora. Climber, creeper.
Pluma. Plume.
    Plumaje. Plumage.
Plumero amarillo. Goldenrod.
Polipodio. Polypody.
    Polipodiacio,-a. Polypodeous.
Portulaca. Purslane.
Prímula, primavera. Cowslip, primrose, polyanthus.
Racimo de flores. Panicle.

R
Raíz. Root.
Ranúnculo. Ranunculus.
Retama. Broom.
Retoño. Shoot, sucker.
Rhamnus. Buckthorn.
Ricino. Castor oil plant.
Risoma. Rhizome.
Roble venenosa. Poison oak.
Rododendro. Rhododendrun.
Rosa. Rose.

Rosa té. Tea rose.

S
Salsolaceo, -a. Salsolaceous.
　　Salsogineo, -a. Salsoginus.
Salvia. Salvia, sage.
Sanguinaria. Bloodroot.
Semilla. Seed.
Sen, sena. Senna.
Sépalo. Sepal.
Seto. Hedge.
　　Seto de boj. Box shrub.
　　Seto vivo o verde. Hedgerow.
Sota. Soaptree.
Suculente. Succulent.

T
Tabaco. Tobacco.
Taco de reina. Nasturtium.
Tallo. Stalk.
Terrón. Sod.
Tornasol. Sunflower.
Totora. Cattail.
Trébol. Clover, trefoil.
Trifolio. Clover, trefoil.
Trillium, trilio. Trillium.
Trinitaria. Bougainvillea.
Trumpet vine. Enredadera de trompeta.
Tulipán. Tulip.
Turba. Moss, peat, peat moss.

V
Vaina. Seed pod.
Variedad. Variety, cultivar.
Varita. Wand.

Vara de oro. Goldenrod.
Vástigo. Scion.
Veigela, veigelia. Weigela.
Verdolaga. Purslane.
Vincapervinca. Periwinkle, vinca.
Vid (uvas). Vine.
Vid kudzu. Kudzu.
Violeta. Violet.

Y
Yaro. Arum.
Yedra. Ivy.

Z
Zanahoria salvaje. Queen Anne's lace.
Zapatilla de dama. Lady's slipper orquid.
Zinnia. Zinnia.
Zumaque. Sumac.
Zumaque venenosa. Poisonwood.

CACTUS Y SUCULENTES
CACTI AND SUCCULENTS

A
Agave. Agave.
Alas de ángel. Bunny ear cactus.
Áloe. Aloe.
Astrofito. Bishop's miter.

B
Biznaga. Barrel cactus.
Biznaga de agua. Candy barrel cactus.

C
Cacto, cactus. Cactus.
Cacto botón. Button cactus.
Cacto cabeza blanca. Cabera cactus.
Cacto de barril. Candy barrel cactus.
Cacto de Lindsay. Lindsay's hedgehog.
Cacto Nido de Pajaro. Bird's nest cactus.
Cactus bola. Ball cactus.
Cactus de lunares. Bunny ear cactus.
Cactus de Navidad. Thanksgiving cactus.
Cactus Estrella. Bishop's cap.
Cactus orquídea. Orchid cactus.
Cactus de erizo. Calico cactus.
Candelabra. Candelabra.
Capa de obispo. Bishop's miter.
Cholla. Cholla, ball cactus.
    Cholla de oso teddy. Teddy-bear cholla.
    Cholla lápiz. Branched pencil cholla.
Cola de castor. Beaver tail cactus.

J
Jarcia. Century plant.

M
Maguey. Maguey.

N
Nopal. Prickly pear.

O
Ocotillo. Ocotillo.
Orejas de conejo. Bunny ear cactus.
Órgano. Saguaro.

P
Pedo de perro. Brain cactus.
Peyote. Peyote.

R
Roca viviente. Living rock.

S
Saguaro. Saguaro.
Succulent. Suculente.

GÉNEROS DE CACTUS Y SUCULENTES
GENERA OF CACTI AND SUCCULENTS

Cactus

Aporocactus
Ariocarpus.
Astrophytum
Cephalocerus
Cereus
Cleistocactus
Copiapoa
Coryphantha
Echinocactus
Echinocereus
Echinopsis
Epiphyllum
Espostoa
Ferocactus
Gymnocalycium
Haageocereus
Hildewinteria
Lobivia
Lophophora
Mammillaria
Matucana
Melocactus
Neobuxbaumia
Neoporteria
Notocactus
Opuntia
Oreocerus
Pachycerus
Parodia
Pilosocereus

Rebutia
Rhipsalis
Sansevieria
Schlumbergia
Stenocactus
Stenocerus
Sulcorebutia
Thelocactus
Trichocerus
Turbinicarpus
Uebelamannia

Suculentes

Adenium
Adromischus
Aeonium
Agave
Aichryson
Aloe
Aloinopsis
Ceropegiea
Conophytum
Cotyledon
Crassula
Dasylirion
Dudleya
Echeveria
Euphorbia
Faucaria
Gasteria
Gibbaeum
Greenovia
Haworthia
Hoya
Huernia

Jatropha
Kalanchoe
Lampranthus
Lithops
Nolina
Pachyphtum
Pachypodium
Pedilanthus
Piaranthus
Pleiospilos
Sansevieria
Sedum
Sempervivum
Senecio
Stomatium
Titanopsis
Trichodiadema
Tylecodon
Yucca

FRUTAS Y VEGETALES
FRUITS AND VEGETABLES

A
Acelga. Chard.
Achicoria. Chicory root.
Alcachofa. Artichoke.
Altramuz. Lupin bean.
Alubia verde. French bean.
Aluvia. Navy bean, white bean.
Angu. Okra.
Apio. Celery.
Aquenio. Achene.
Arándano. Cranberry.
Arándano azul. Blueberry.
Arúgula. Arugula.

B
Banana. Banana.
Baya. Berry.
Berro. Cress, watercress.
Berza. Collard, kale.
Betabel. Beet.
Berenjena. Aubergine, eggplant.
Brócol, broccoli. Broccoli.

C
Cafeto. Coffee bush.
Calabaza. Pumpkin, gourd.
Calabacita, calabacín. Squash, zucchini, marrow, courgette.
Camote. Sweet potato, yam.
Cantalopo. Cantaloupe, muskmelon.
Cebolla. Onion.
Chalota, chalote. Shallot.

Champiñon. Mushroom.
Chícharo. Pea.
Chili. Chile pepper.
Chirivía. Parsnip.
Ciruela. Plum.
Coco. Coconut.
Col. Cabbage.
Col de Brusela. Brussel sprout.
Col risado. Kale.
Coliflor. Cauliflower.
Colirrábano. Kohlrabi.

D
Durazno. Peach.

E
Ejote. Green bean.
Elote. French bean.
Endibia, endivia. Chicory, endive.
Escorzonera. Salisfy.
Espárrago. Asparagus.
Espinaca. Spinach.
Espora. Spore.

F
Frambuesa. Raspberry.
Fresa. Strawberry.
Frijol. Bean.
    Frijol de cera. Wax vean.
    Frijol negro. Black bean.
Fruta. Fruit.

G
Granada china. Passion fruit.
Grano. Kernel.
Guayaba. Guava.

H

Haba amarilla de cera. Wax bean.
Haba de lima. Butter bean, Lima bean.
Híbrido. Hybrid.
Higo. Fig.

J

Jitomate. Tomato.

K

Kiwi. Kiwi.

L

Lechuga. Lettuce.
Legumbre. Legume.
Lima, limón verde. Lime.
Limón. Lemon.

M

Maduro, -a. Ripe.
    Madurar. To ripen.
Maíz. Corn.
    Maíz dulce. Sweet corn.
Mandarina. Mandarina orange.
Manzana. Apple.
Maracuyá. Passion fruit.
Melón. Cantaloupe.
Melón chino. Honeydew melón.
Membrillo. Quince.
Mora. Blackberry, mulberry.
Mora azul. Blueberry.

N

Naba. Rutabega.
Nabo. Parsnip, turnip.
Naranja. Orange.

Nectarina. Nectarine.
Níspera. Loquat, medlar.
Ocra. Okra.

P
Papa. Potato.
Pastinaco. Parsnip.
Pávia. Nectarine.
Pepino. Cucumber.
Pera. Pear.
Piña. Pineapple.
Pimiento. Capsicum, pepper, bell pepper, sweet pepper.
    Pimiento amarillo. Banana pepper.
    Pimiento rojo. Cherry pepper.
Plátano. Banana.
Plátano macho. Plantain.
Pomelo. Grapefruit.
Poro, puerro. Leek

R
Rábano. Radish.
Reliquia. Heirloom (e.g. heirloom tomato).
Rizoma. Rhizome.
Ruibarbo. Rhubarb.

S
Sandía. Watermelon.
Semilla. Seed.
Soya. Soybean.

T
Tangerina. Tangerine.
Típica. Heirloom (e.g. heirloom tomato).
Tomatito cherry. Cherry tomato.
Tomatillo. Green tomato.
Toronja. Grapefruit.

Tradicional. Heirloom (e.g. heirloom tomato).
Tubérculo. Tuber.

U
Uva. Grape.

V
Vegetal. Vegetable.

Y
Yuca. Yucca.

Z
Zanahoria. Carrot.
Zarzamora. Blackberry.

HIERBAS/HERBS

A
Abesón. Dill.
Acedera, agrilla. Sorrel.
Ajedrea. Savory.
Ajo. Garlic.
Amaranto. Amaranth.
Anís. Anise.
Albahaca. Basil.
Asperilla. Woodruff.

B
Borraja. Borage.

C
Cebolleta, cebollino. Chives.
Cilantro. Cilantro.
Clavo. Clove.

E
Eneldo. Dill.
Estragón. Tarragon.

G
Galio. Woodruff.

H
Hierba. Herb.
Hierba de limón. Citronella.
Hierba luisa. Citronella, chamomile, lemon verbena.
Hierbabuena. Spearmint.
Hinojo. Fennel.
Hisopo. Hyssop.
Hoja de laurel. Bay leaf.

L
Lavanda. Lavender.
Limoncillo. Chamomile.
Matricaria. Feverfew.

M
Mejorana. Marjoram.
Menta. Mint.
Mostaza. Mustard.

O
Oregano. Oregano.

P
Perejil. Parsley.
Perifollo. Chervil.

R
Romero. Rosemary.

S
Salvia. Sage.
Santa maría. Feverfew.

T
Tomillo. Thyme.

Z
Zacate de limón. Citronella.

ÁRBOLES/TREES

A
Abedul. Birch.
Abeto. Fir.
    Abeto balsámico. Balsam fir.
    Abeto blanco. Silver or white fir.
Acacia. Acacia.
Acacia blanca. Locust.
Acajú. Cashew tree.
Álamo. Poplar.
    Álamo blanco. White poplar.
    Álamo negro. Black poplar.
Álamo temblón. Aspen.
Alcornoque. Cork tree.
Alerce. Larch.
Algarroba. Carob tree.
Algarrobo. Locust.
Aliso. Alder.
Almendro. Almond.
Anacardo marañón. Cashew tree.
Árbol. Tree.
Árbol de hoja perenne (n.), de hoja perenne (adj.)
Evergreen.
Árbol Joshua. Joshua tree.
Arce. Maple.
Avellano. Hazel or hazelnut tree.

B
Balsa. Balso.
Banano. Banana tree.
Bergamota. Bergamot.
Boj, boje. Boxwood.

C

Caducifolio, -a. Deciduous.
Canelo. Cinnemon tree.
Caoba. Mahogany.
Carpe. Hornbeam.
Casia. Cassia.
Castaño. Chestnut tree.
Cedro. Cedar.
Ceiba. Ceiba.
Cerezo. Cherry tree.
Ciprés. Cypress.
Ciruelo. Plum tree.
Cítrico (n.), cítrico, -a (adj.). Citrus.
Cocotero. Coconut tree.
Conifera. Conífer.
    Conífero, -a. Coniferous.
Cornejo. Dogwood.
Corozo. Corozo palm.
Corteza. Bark.

D

Datilero. Date palm.
Duraznero. Peach tree.

E

Ébono. Ebony.
Encinillo. Scrub oak.
Encino. Oak.
Eucalipto. Eucaliptus.

F

Feijoa. Feijoa.
Fresno. Ash.

G

Guayabo. Guava tree.

H
Haya. Beech.
Higuera. Fig tree.

J
Jabí. Ironwood.
Jacarandá. Jacaranda.
Junipero. Juniper.

L
Lárice. Larch.
Laurel. Laurel.
Limero. Lime tree.
Limonero. Lemon tree.
Liquidámber americano. Sweet gum tree.

M
Magnolia. Magnolia.
Malva. Mallow tree.
Manglar. Mangrove.
Manzana silvestre. Crab apple.
Manzano. Apple tree.
Membrillo, membrillero. Quince tree.
Miraguano. Kapok tree.
Moral. Mulberry tree.

N
Naranjo. Orange tree.
Níspero. Loquat or medlar tree.
Nogal. Walnut or tree.
Nogal Americano. Hickory tree.

O
Ocote. Montezuma pine.
Olivo. Olive tree.
Olmo. Elm.

Oxidendro. Sorrel tree.

P

Pacana. Hickory or pecan tree.

Palma caruta, de cerdos, de grana o de yagua. Royal palm, mountain-cabbage.

Palma chit. Thatch palm.

Palma llanera. Fan palm.

Palmera. Palm.

Palmera enana. Palmetto.

Palmito. Fan palm, palmetto.

Palo blanco. Palo blanco.

Palo Brasil, palo de agua, palo de Brasil. Brazilwood.

Palo brea. Palo brea.

Palo fierro. Ironwood.

Palo verde. Palo verde.

Pata de elefante. Ponytail palm.

Pejibaye. Peach palm.

Peral. Pear tree.

Pícea. Spruce.

> **Pícea azul.** Blue spruce.
>
> **Pícea blanca.** White spruce.
>
> **Pícea roja.** Red spruce.

Piña. Pine cone.

Pino. Pine.

> **Pino amarillo o ponderosa.** Ponderosa pine.
>
> **Pino rojo.** Norway or red pine.
>
> **Pino blanco.** White pine.

Piñon. Pinyon tree.

Platanero. Banana tree.

Pomelo. Grapefruit tree.

Q

Quinito. Kumquat tree.

R

Rama. Branch, tree limb.
Ramita. Twig.
Robinia. Locust.
Roble, encino. Oak.
  Roble americano, boreal o rojo. Red oak.
  Roble blanco. White oak.
  Roble siempre verde. Live oak.

S

Sabuco, saúco. Elderberry.
Sagú. Sago palm.
Sauce. Willow.
Savia. Sap.
Sasafrás. Sassafras.
Sequoia. Secoya, secuoya, redwood.
Setos. Boxwood.
Sicóromo, sicoromo. Sycamore.

T

Teca. Teak.
Tejo. Yew.
Tilo. Basswood, linden.
Tupelo. Tupelo.

JARDÍN, INVERNADERO Y VIVERO

GARDEN, GREENHOUSE & NURSERY

A

Abeja. Bee.
Abono. Mulch.
Acceso. Driveway.
Acento. Accent.
Acidez. Acidity.
   Acídico, -a. Acídic.
Acristalamiento. Glazing.
Acuático, -a. Aquatic.
Adaptación. Adaptation.
   Adaptarse. To adapt.
Afilar. To hone or sharpen.
Agua. Water.
Aire condicionado. Air conditioning.
Albañilería. Masonry.
   Albañil, -a. Mason.
Alcalino, -a. Alkaline.
Alero. Eave.
Alimentación. Feeding.
Alumbrado. Lighting.
Aluminio. Aluminum.
Allanar. To grade.
Ambiente. Environment.
   Ambiental. Environmental.
Ambulante. Gradient.
Amonio. Ammonium.
A nivel. Level.
A nivel más bajo, al ras de suelo. Sunken.
Aplanar. To grade.
   Aplanamiento. Grading.

Aplicación. Application.
    Aplicar. To apply.
Arar. To till.
Arco. Arch.
Arenilla. Grit.
Armazón. Frame, framework.
Artificial. Artificial.
Atrio. Atrium.
Azotea. Terrace, rooftop terrace.

B
Bajada de aguas. Downspout.
Balcón. Balcony.
Banca, banco. Bench.
Barda. Fence.
Barro. Clay.
Base. Base, footing.
Berma. Berm.
Biodegradable. Biodegradable.
Bodega. Storeroom.
Boiler. Boiler.
Borde. Edge.
Bordillo. Curb.
Bosque. Woodland.
    Del bosque. Woodland.
Bushel. Bushel.

C
Cable. Electrical cable.
Calcio. Calcium.
Calentador, caldera, calefón. Boiler.
Caliente. Hot.
Calor. Heat.
    Pérdida de calor. Heat loss.
Calle. Street.

Callejón, callejuela. Alley.

Camino. Road.

Campo. Field.

Canal. Channel.

Canaleta, canalón. Gutter.

Cantero, -a. Stonemason.

Capa de agua. Water table.

Capacidad. Capacity.

Captan. Captan.

Casa. House.

Carpintero, -a. Carpenter.

Cenador. Bower.

Cenegal. Bog.

Ceniza. Ash.

Cerca. Fence.

    Cerca de madera. Picket fence.

Certificado, -a. Certified.

    Certificar. To certify.

Césped. Lawn.

Chimenea. Chimney.

Ciénaga. Bog, marsh, swamp.

Cimientos. Foundation.

Circulación. Circulation.

Cisterna. Cistern.

Cobertizo. Shed, lean-to.

Cobertura de suelo. Groundcover.

Codigo. Code.

Coger. To pick.

Color. Color.

Columna. Column.

Combustible. Fuel (e.g. gasolina).

Comedero de pájaros. Bird feeder.

Compost. Compost.

    Mezcla de compost sin tierra. Soilless compost mixture.

Compuesta. Compound.

Comunidad de plantas. Plant community.

Condensación. Condensation.

Condición. Condition.

Confín. Abutment.

Conservatorio. Conservatory.

Construcción. Construction.

    Constructor, -a. Builder.

    Construir. To construct.

Construcción de piedra. Stonework.

Contacto. Electrical outlet.

Contenedor. Container.

Contractor. Contractor.

Control. Control.

Controlador. Controller.

Contorno. Contour.

Corriente. Electrical current; draft, draught.

Corriente de convección. Convection current.

Cortafuego, -s. Firebreak.

Cortar. To cut or mow.

Cortavientos. Windbreak.

Cosecha. Harvest, crop.

    Cosechar. To harvest.

Cultivar. Variedad.

Cultivo. Crop, cultivation.

    Cultivar. To cultivate, grow or till.

D

Declive. Pitch of a roof.

Decorativo, -a. Ornamental, decorative.

Deficiencia. Deficiency.

Depósito. Shed.

Desagüe. Drainage.

    Desaguar. To drain.

    Tubo de desagüe. Drainpipe.

Dibujos. Plans.
Dimensión. Dimension.
Dióxido de carbón. Carbon dioxide.
Directo, -a. Direct.
Diseño. Design.
    Diseñar. To design.
Diversidad. Diversity.
División. Division.
Domo. Dome.
Dominante. Dominant.
Dosel. Canopy.
Drenaje. Drain.
    Drenar. To drain.
Duro, -a. Hard.

E
Ecosistema. Ecosystem.
Electricidad. Electricity, luz.
    Eléctrico, -a. Electric.
    Eléctrico, -a, electrecista. Electrician.
Elevación. Elevation.
Elevado, -a. Raised.
Empapado. Drenched.
    Empapar. To drench.
Emparrado. Bower.
Encintado. Curb.
Enrejado. Trellis, grate, grille.
Entablado. Boardwalk.
Entorno. Environment.
Entrada. Entrance, driveway.
Época de cultivo. Growing season.
Equipo. Equipment, work crew.
Erosión. Erosion.
Escalón. Stair, step.
Estandardización. Standardization.

Escape. Leak.
Escurrirse. To trickle.
Espacio. Space.
Especie. Species.
Espesor. Thickness.
Esqueje. Cutting, scion.
Estación. Season.
Estanque. Pond, pool.
Estante. Shelf.
Estiércol. Manure.
Estirilización. Sterilization.
Estructura. Building, structure.
Excavación. Excavation.
    Excavar. To excavate or dig.
Extranjero, -a. Alien.

F
Fauna silvestre. Wildlife.
Fertilizante. Fertilizer.
    Fertilización. Fertilization, enrichment.
Filtración. Seepage out.
Floríféreo, -a. Floriferous.
Flujo de aire. Air flow.
Follaje. Foliage.
Foreano, -a. Alien.
Formaldehído. Formaldehyde.
Fosfato. Phosphate.
Fósforo. Phosphorus.
Fotoperiódico, -a. Photoperiodic.
Fotosintesis. Photosynthesis.
Fresco, -a. Cool.
Frío (n.), frío, -a (adj.) Cold.
Fuente. Fountain.
Fuego. Fire.
Fuga. Leak, seepage in.

Fumigación. Fumigation.
  Fumigar. Fumigate.
Fungicida. Fungicide.

G

Galera. Arcade, veranda.
Garaje. Garage.
Geodésico, -a. Geodesic.
Germinación. Germination.
  Germinar. To germinate.
Gotera. Leak.
Gravilla. Grit.

H

Herbicida. Herbicide.
Hibernación. Hibernation.
  Hibernar. To hibernate.
Hidroponía. Hydroponics.
  Hidropónico, -a. Hydroponic.
Hilada de ladrillos. Course of bricks.
Hilera. Row.
Húmedo, -a. Damp.
Humididad. Humidity.
Humus. Humus.

I

Iluminación. Illumination, lighting.
Impermeable. Waterproof.
Inclinación. Gradient.
Injerto. Grafting.
  Injertar. To graft.
Inmueble. Building.
Insoluble. Insoluble.
Inverdadero. Greenhouse.

J

Jardín. Garden.
> **Jardín botánico.** Botanical garden.
> **Jardín comunitario.** Community garden.
> **Jardinero, -a.** Gardener.

L

Labrar. To till.
Linde. Abutment.
Liso, -a. Smooth.
Listón. Lath, slat.
Loam. Loam.
Losa. Cement slab.
Lote. Lot.
Lumen. Lumen.
Luz. Light, electricity.
Luz suplementaria. Supplementary light.

M

Maceta. Pot.
> **Maceta de barro.** Clay plot.
> **Maceta para barandilla, maceta de balcón.**
> Windowbox.
Macizo. Bed, flower bed.
Madera. Timber.
Maduro, -a. Mature, ripe, old.
> **Madurar.** To mature or ripen.
Magnesio. Magnesium.
Manganeso. Manganese.
Manguera, manga. Hosepipe.
Mantamiento. Maintenance.
Mantillo. Mulch.
Marco. Frame.
Marquesina. Awning.
Mastique, masilla. Putty.

Materia prima o bruta. Raw materials.
Maya ciclónica. Cyclone fence.
Mecanismo. Mechanism.
Medida. Measurement, size.
Mezcla. Compound, mixture.
> **Mezclar.** To mix.
Mezcla para macetas. Potting mix.
Mojado, -a. Wet.
Monitor. Monitor.
Monocultura. Monoculture.
Muro. Wall.
> **Muro de retén.** Retaining wall.

N
Natural. Natural.
Naturaleza. Nature.
Nido. Bird nest.
Nitrato. Nitrate.
> **Nitrato de amonio.** Ammonium nitrate.
> **Nitrato de potasio.** Potassium nitrate.
Nitrógeno. Nitrogen.
Nivelación. Grading.
Nivelado, -a. Level.
Nivel hidrostático. Water table.
Nuevo, -a. New.
Nutriente. Nutrient.
> **Nutrición.** Nutrition.

O
Olor. Odor, smell.
Orgánico, -a. Organic.
Organofósoro, -a. Organophosphorus.
Oxigenar. To oxygenate.

P
Paisajismo. Landscaping.

Pajarera. Birdhouse.

Panel. Panel.

Pantano. Bog, marsh, swamp, wetland.

Pared. Wall.

 Pared divisoria. Partition wall.

Parte. Part.

Parterre. Bed, flower bed, border, edge.

Patio. Courtyard, yard.

Patrón. Pattern.

Pavimentación. Paving.

Pedestal. Pedestal.

Pendiente. Gradient, pitch of a roof.

Perfil. Contour.

Pérgola. Pergola.

Persiana. Louvre.

Perspectiva. Perspective.

Pesticida. Pesticide.

pH. pH.

Pie. Footing.

Pisar. To tamp.

 Tierra apisonada. Tamped earth.

Planeación. Planning.

 Planear. To plan.

 Planes. Plans.

Plantar. To plant.

 Plantar en maceta. To pot.

Plástico (n.), plástico,-a (adj.). Plastic.

Plataforma. Platform.

Plaza. Plaza.

Plomería. Plumbing.

Poda. Pruning.

 Podar. To prune or crop.

Polinación. Pollination.

 Polinar. To pollinate.

Pórtico. Porch, portico.

Portabilidad. Portability.

Posición. Position.

Potasa. Potash.

Potasio. Potassium.

Pozo para hacer fuego. Fire pit.

Pradera. Grassland.

Prado. Field, lawn, meadow.

Preserva (lugar). Preserve.

Privacidad, privación. Privacy.

Producto químico. Chemical.

Propagación. Propagation.

> **Propagador.** Propagator.

Propiadad. Property.

Protegido. Sheltered.

Proyecto. Project.

Pudrimiento. Rot.

> **Pudrido, -a.** Rotted.

> **Pudrir.** To rot.

Puerta. Door.

Pulverized. Pulverizado, -a.

Q
Químico, -a (adj.) Chemical.

R
Rampa. Ramp.

Recoger. To gather.

Reflectador. Reflector.

Regar. To water.

Reja. Grate, grille, gate, fence post, pale.

Reloj. Clock.

Reparación. Repair, repairing.

> **Reparar.** To repair.

Requerir. Require.

Resguardado, -a. Sheltered.

Resistente. Hardy.
Respiración. Resperation.
Retrasado, -a. Stunted.
Riachuelo. Rivulet.
Ribereño, -a. Riparian.
Riego. Watering.
Robusto, -a. Hardy.
Rocio. Mist, spray.
    Rociar. To mist or spray.
Rompevientos. Windbreak.

S
Sabana. Savanna.
Sano, -a. Healthy.
Sección. Section.
Seco, -a. Dry.
    Secar. To dry.
Seguridad. Security.
Semilla. Seed.
Sembrado. Field.
Sembrar. To plant or sow.
Sendero. Path.
Sensor. Sensor.
Separación. Division.
Seto. Hedge.
Siembra. Planting.
Sistema. System.
Sitio. Site.
    Orentación de sitio. Site orientation.
    In situ. Site-specific.
Sol. Sun.
    Soleado, -a. Sunny.
Solar. Solar.
    Energía solar. Solar energy.
    Luz solar. Sunlight.

Radiación solar. Solar radiation.

Solería, solado. Flooring.

Sólido, -a. Solid.

Sombra. Shade.

Sombreado, -a. Shady.

Subterráneo, -a. Underground.

Succesión. Succesion.

Suave. Soft.

Suelo. Floor.

Suelto, -a. Loose, soft.

Sulfato. Sulphate.

Sumidero. Drain.

Surco. Furrow.

Superficie. Surfice.

Sustancia química. Chemical.

T

Tabla. Board.

Tablero. Panel.

Taller. Workshop.

Tamaño. Size.

Tanque de almacenamiento. Storage tank.

Techo. Roof, rooftop terrace.

Tejado. Roof.

Temperatura. Temperature.

Temporada. Season.

Temporado, -a. Temperate.

Temporada de cultivo. Growing season.

Termómetro. Thermometer.

Termostato. Thermostat.

Terraza. Terrace.

Terreno. Ground, terrain.

Tierra. Dirt, ground, soil.

Tierra apisonada. Rammed earth, tamped earth.

Toldo. Awning.

Tolerante. Tolerant.
Topiaria. Topiary.
Topografía. Topography.
Toxicidad. Toxicity.
Tragaluz. Skylight.
Trasluciente. Translucent.
Transparente. Transparent.
Transpiración. Transpiration.
Tratamiento. Treatment.
Tropical. Tropical.
Tubo. Pipe.
Tubo de ventilación. Air duct.

V
Vacio, -a. Hollow.
Vapor. Steam.
>   **Vapor de agua.** Water vapor.
Ventana. Window.
Ventilación. Ventilation.
>   **Conducto o rejilla de ventilación.** Vent.
>   **Ventilado, -a.** Ventilated.
Ventilador. Ventilator.
Veranda. Veranda.
Vermiculita. Vermiculite.
Vidriado. Glazing.
Vidrio. Glass.
Vida salvaje. Wildlife.
Viejo, -a. Old.
Vista. View.
Vivero. Nursery.
Voltaje. Voltage.

Z
Zapata. Footing.
Zona. Zone.

HERRAMIENTAS, MATERIALES Y FERRETERÍA
TOOLS, MATERIALS AND HARDWARE

A
Accesorio. Attachment.
Acople, cople, conexión. Coupling.
Adoquín. Cobblestone, paving stone.
Afilador. Sharpener.
Agregado. Aggregate.
Aireador. Aerator.
Aislamiento. Insulation.
    Aislado, -a. Insulated.
    Aislar. To insulate.
Alambre. Wire.
    Alambre de púas. Barbed wire.
Alimentador. Feeder.
Aljibe. Water tank.
Alicates. Pliers, tongs.
Almádana, almádena. Sledge hammer.
Alto volumen. High pressure.
Amarra. Rope.
Amolador. Sharpener, whetstone.
Arena. Sand.
Arpillera. Burlap, hessian.
Aserrar. To saw.
Aspersor. Sprinkler.
Azada. Hoe.
Azulejo. Tile.

B
Bajo volumen. Low pressure.
Baldosa. Tile.
Banca de trabajo. Work bench.

Barra. Metal bar or rod.

Barreno. Auger.

Barreta. Bar, pry bar.

Biombo. Screen (partition).

Bieldo. Pitchfork.

Bisagra. Hinge.

Bloque. Block.

    Bote o contenedor de basura. Trash can.

Bola. Ball.

Bolsa. Bag.

Bomba. Pump.

    Bomba sumergible. Submergible pump.

    Bomba de agua. Water pump.

    Bombear. To pump.

Bombillo. Light bulb.

Bordeadora. Edger.

Bote o contenedor de basura. Garbage or rash can.

Bramante. Twine.

Brida. Clamp.

Broca. Drill bit.

Bulldozer. Bulldozer.

C

Cable. Cable, wire.

Cadena. Chain.

Caja. Box.

Cal. Lime.

Calefactor. Heater.

    Calefacción. Heating.

Camión. Truck.

Canasta. Basket.

Cargador frontal. Front-end loader.

Cargo. Load.

Carretilla. Wheelbarrow.

Cavador. Fence post digger, post hole digger.

Cemento. Cement.

Caja o centro de cargo. Power supply box.

Cepillo. Brush.

Cinta. Tape.

> **Cinta eléctrica.** Electrical tape.
>
> **Cinta masking.** Masking tape.
>
> **Cinta teflón.** Teflon tape.

Cizalla. Sheers, wire cutters.

Clavija. Peg.

Clavo. Nail.

Coladera. Filter.

Compresora. Compressor.

Concreto. Concrete.

Conector, conectador. Connector.

Contador de agua. Water meter.

Contenador. Bin.

Contenedor de basura. Trash can.

Cople, conexión. Coupling.

Cordel. Cord, twine.

Cortaalambres. Wire cutter.

Cortacirculos. Hole saw.

Cortadora de malezas. Weed cutter, weed whacker.

Cuba, cubo. Tub.

Cubeta. Bucket.

Cuchillo. Knife.

Cuerda. Cord, rope, twine.

Charola. Tray.

Chiflón. Nozzle.

D

Debastadora. Trimmer.

Desarmador, destornillador. Screwdriver.

> **Desarmador estandard.** Flathead screwdriver.
>
> **Desarmador Phillips o de cruz.** Phillips screwdriver.

Desbrozadora. Brush or weed cutter, weed whacker.
Desparramador. Sower.

E
Enlistonado. Lath.
Escala. Ladder.
Escoba. Broom.
Escuadra. Carpenter's square.
Espaciador. Spacer.
Espejo. Mirror.
Estaca. Stake.
Excavadora. Excavator.
Extendadora. Spreader.
Extensión. Extension.
Extensor. Extender.

F
Ferretería. Hardware.
Fibra de vidrio. Fibreglass.
Filtro. Filter.
Foco. Light bulb.
Forro. Liner.
Fregadora. Sink.

G
Gancho. Hanger, hook.
Generador. Generator.
Grúa. Crane.
Guantes. Gloves.
Guía. Guide

H
Hacha. Ax, axe.
Herramienta. Tool.
    Caja de herramientas. Tool box.
Hierro. Iron.

Hierro colado. Cast iron.

> **Hierro forjado o labrado.** Wrought iron.

Hilo. Line.

Hoja de sierra. Saw blade.

Humedecedor. Humidifier.

Intercambiador de calor. Heat exchanger.

I

Interior. Liner.

J

Jeringa. Syringe.

Juego de (e.g. juego de llaves). Set of (e.g. set of wrenches).

L

Ladrillo. Brick.

Lámina. Sheet metal, corrugated metal.

Lápiz. Pencil.

Lavabo. Sink.

Lazo. Cord.

Limpiador. Cleaner.

Líquido (n.). Liquid.

> **Líquido, -a. (adj.)** Liquid

Listón. Lath

Lona. Tarp.

Losa. Paving stone.

Llanta. Wheel.

Llave. Faucet, key, wrench.

> **Llave adjustable.** Adjustable wrench.
>
> **Llave fostada.** Crescent wrench.
>
> **Llave de dado.** Socket wrench.

M

Maceta. Pot.

> **Maceta de turba.** Peat pot.

Macetero. Planter.
Machete. Machete.
Madera. Wood.
Madera contrachapada o terciada. Plywood.
Malacate. Winch.
Mangera. Hose.
   Mangera flexible. Flexible hose.
Mango. Handle, shank.
Máquina. Machine.
Marro. Maul, sledge hammer.
Martillo. Hammer.
Materiales de construcción. Building materials.
Matraca. Socket wrench.
Maya. Screen (wire mesh).
Mazo. Mallet.
Mensula. Bracket.
Merchero. Jet.
Mesa. Table.
Metal ondulado. Corrugated metal.
Metro. Ruler.
Mezcladora. Mixer.
Mini-cargador. Bobcat.
Montoniveladora. Grader.
Mosquitero. Screen (wire mesh), screen window.
Motor. Motor.
Motosierra. Chainsaw.
Muela. Jaw of a wrench.

N
Navaja. Knife.

O
Orejera. Ear muffs.
Orilladora. Edger.

P

Paja. Straw, thatch.
Pala. Shovel.
Pala hidráulica. Hydraulic shovel.
Palanca. Pry bar.
Pavimentadora. Paver.
Perlita. Perlite.
Peso. Weight, load.
Pico. Pick, pickax.
Pintura. Paint.
Pinza de punta. Needle-nose pliers.
Pinzas. Pliers.
Pisón. Rammer.
Plástico (n.). Plastic;
    Plástico, -a (adj.). Plastic.
Plug. Plug.
Polyietileno. Polythene.
Podadera. Pruning shears.
Poste. Fence post.
Prensa. Clamp.
Presión. Pressure.
    Alta presión. High pressure.
    Baja presión. Low pressure.
Presurizado, a. Pressurized.
    Presurizar. To pressurize.
Pulea. Pulley.
PVC. PVC.

R

Rastrillo. Rake.
Red. Net.
Reata. Rope.
Regadora. Watering can.
Repuesto. Replacement.
Retracil. Utility knife.

Retroexcavadora. Backhoe.
Revestimiento. Liner.
Revolvadora. Cement mixer.
Rociador. Sprayer.
Rodillera. Knee pad.
Rollo. Roll.
Rollo de hule o plástico. Plastic sheeting.
Roller. Roller.
Rueda. Wheel.

S
Sacar con una bomba. To pump.
Sembradora. Planter (machine), sower.
Serrar. To saw.
Serrote, serucho. Handsaw.
Sierra. Saw.
    Sierra de abrazadera. Rip saw.
    Sierra arco. Bow saw, hack saw.
    Sierra de mano. Handsaw.
    Sierra de metals. Hack saw.
Sonda. Auger.
Sistema. System.
Sopladora. Leaf blower.
Sutidor. Jet.

T
Tabicón, tabique. Cinder block.
Tabla. Board.
Tablilla. Shingle.
Tablón. Plank.
Tanque. Tank.
    Tanque de almacenamiento. Storage tank.
    Tanque de agua. Water tank.
Tapa. Plug.
Teja. Roof tile.
Temporizador. Timer.

Tenazas. Pincers, pliers, tongs.
Terracotta. Terra cota.
Tierra. Dirt, earth.
Tierra apisonada. Rammed earth.
Tiesto. Planter.
Tijera de podar. Pruning shears.
Tijeras. Scissors.
Tinaco. Water tank.
Tornillo. Screw.
Torno de mano. Clamp.
Tractor. Tractor.
Trampa. Trap.
Trapo. Rag.
Triplay, triplex. Plywood.
Tubo. Tube.
    Tubería. Tubing.
Tuerca. Nut.

U
Unión. Connector.

V
Válvula. Valve.
    Válvula esférica. Globe or spherical valve.
    Válvula de seguridad. Safety valve.
Ventilador. Ventilator.
Vibrador. Vibrator.
Viga, vigueta. Joist, beam.
Vinilo. Vinyl.
Volquete. Dump truck.

Y
Yute. Burlap.

Z
Zapapico. Pickaxe.

TIPOS DE PIEDRA
TYPES OF STONE

A
Aspersón. Sandstone.

B
Basalto. Basalt.

C
Calcedonia. Chert.
Caliza. Limestone.
Cantera. Quarry.
Cuartzo. Quartz.

E
Enlosado. Flagstone.
Esquito. Schist.

G
Gabro. Gabbro.
Gneis. Gneiss.
Granito. Granite.
Grava, gravilla. Gravel.
Guijarro. Pebble.

M
Mármol. Marble.
Mármol travertino. Travertine.

O
Ónix, ónice. Onyx.

P
Pedernal. Chert.
Piedra. Rock, Stone.

Piedra pómez. Pumice.
Piedrecita, piedrita. Pebble.
Pirita. Firestone.
Pizzara. Slate.

T
Toba calcárea. Tufa.

COLORES/COLORS

A
Aguamarina. Aquamarine, blue Green.
Alabastrino. Alabaster.
Amarillo, -a. Yellow.
Anaranjado, -a; de color naranjo. Orange.
Azul. Blue.
    Azul celeste. Sky blue.
    Azul cielo o claro. Powder blue.
    Azul marino. Navy blue.
    Azul de medianoche, azul oscuro. Midnight blue.
    Azul de ultramar. Ultramarine.
    Azul metálico. Steel blue.
    Azul verdoso. Aquamarine, blue green.

B
Beige, beis. Beige, buff.
Blanco, -a. White.
Bermellón. Burgundy, vermilion.
Borgoño. Burgundy.
Burdeos. Garnet.

C
Café. Brown.
Cardenillo. Verdigris.
Carmesí. Crimson.
Carmín. Carmine.
Castaño. Brown.
Castaño claro. Sorrel.
Castaño rojizo. Auburn, russet.
Celeste perlado. Powder blue.
Cerúleo. Cerulean.
Cobrizo, -a. Copper.
Color. Color.
Color crema. Cream.

Color salmón. Salmon.
Coral. Coral.

D
Dorado, -a. Gold.

E
Ébono. Ebony.
Escarlata. Scarlet.

G
Granate. Garnet.
Gris. Gray, grey.
    Gris oscuro, gris pizarra. Slate gray.
    Gris paloma. Dove gray.
    Gris plateado. Silver gray.
    Gris topo. Taupe.
Guinda. Oxblood.

L
Lavanda, lila. Lavender.

M
Malva. Mauve.
Marfil. Ivory.
Marrón. Brown.
    Marrón oscura. Umber.
    Marrón oliva. Drab.
    Marrón rojizo. Russet.
    Marrón topo. Taupe.
Matiz. Shade.
Multicolor. Variegated.

N
Negro, -a. Black.

O

Ocre. Ochre, umber.

P

Pardo. Dun.
Platiado, -a. Silver, silver gray.
Purpúreo. Purple.
Purpúreo rojizo. Magenta.

R

Rayado, -a. Striped.
Rojo, -a. Red.
 Rojo oscuro. Oxblood.
Rosa. Pink.

S

Siena. Sienna.

T

Teja. Rust.
Tono. Shade.
Trasluciente. Translucent.
Turquesa. Turquoise.

U

Ultramarino, ultramaro. Ultramarine.

V

Variado, -a. Variegated.
Variegación. Variegation.
Verde. Green.
 Verde azul, verdiazul. Blue green.
 Verde bosque. Forest green.
 Verde brillante. Kelly green.
 Verde esmeralda. Emerald green, viridian.
 Verde musgo. Moss green.

Verde oscuro. Hunter green.
Verde turquesa. Jade green.
Verdín, cardenillo. Verdigris.
Violeta. Violet, purple.

ESTACIONES DEL AÑO, MESES, EL DÍA, DIRECCIONES
SEASONS, MONTHS, THE DAY, DIRECTIONS

Estaciones/Seasons

Primavera. Spring.
Verano. Summer.
Otoño. Autumn, fall.
Invierno. Winter.

Calendario: Meses/Calendar: Months.

Enero. January.
Febrero. February.
Marzo. March.
Abril. April.
Mayo. May.
Junio. June.
Julio. July.
Agosto. August.
Septiembre. September.
Octubre. October.
Noviembre. November.
Diciembre. December.

El día/The day.

Amanecer, alba. Dawn.
Mañana. Morning.
Mediodía. Midday, noon.
Tarde. Aftenoon.
   Atardecer. Late afternoon.
Del atardecer, por la tarde, tarde. Evening.
Noche. Night.

Direcciones. Directions.

Norte. North.
> **Nor (adj.), hacia el norte.** North (in the direction of).
> **Noreste.** Northeast.
> **Noroeste.** Northwest.

Sur. South.
> **Sur (adj.), hacia el sur.** South (in the direction of).
> **Sureste.** Southeast.
> **Suroeste.** Southwest.

Este. East.
> **Del este (adj.), hacia el este.** East (in the direction of).

Oeste. West.
> **Del oeste (adj.), al oeste.** West (in the direction of).

MEDIDAS Y DIMENSIONES
MEASUREMENTS AND DIMENSIONS

A
Acre. Acre.
Altura. Heigth.
    Alto, -a. High.
Ambulante. Gradient.
Anchura. Width.
    Ancho, -a. Wide.
Ángulo. Angle.
    Angular. Ángular.
Área. Area.

C
Calculation. Cálculo.
Calidad. Quality.
Cantidad. Quantity.
Capacidad. Capacity.
Celsio. Celsius.
Centro. Center.
Centímetro. Centimeter.
Círculo. Circle.
    Circular. Circular.
Circunferencia. Circumference.
Circunscribir. Circumscribe.
Cuadra (n.); cuadrado, -a (adj.). Square.
Cúbico, -a. Cubic.

D
Decimal. Decimal.
Derecho, -a. Right, straight.
Diametro. Diameter.
Dimensión. Dimension.
Distancía. Distance.

Docena. Dozen.

C
Cantidad. Quantity.

E
Equidistante. Equidistant.
Escala. Scale (i.e. dimensional).
Espesor. Thickness.
Estimación. Estimation.
Estimar. To estimate. .
Externo, -a. External, outside.

F
Fahreinheit. Fahreinheit.

G
Galón. Gallon.
Grado. Degree.
Gráfica. Graphic.
Grueso. Thickness.
Hectárea. Hectare.

H
Horizontal. Horizontal.

I
Inclinación. Gradient.
Interno, -a. Inner.
Izquierdo, -a. Left.

K
Kilo, kilogramo. Kilogram.

L
Lado. Side.
Lateral. Lateral.

Largura. Length.
  Largo, -a. Long.
Libra. Pound.
Limite. Límit.
Lineal. Linear.
Litro. Liter.

M
Máximo. Maximum.
Medida. Measurement.
  Medir. To measure.
Medio. Average.
Metro. Meter.
  Metro cuadrado. Square meter.
  Metro cúbito. Cubic meter.
Milímetro. Millimeter.
Mínimo. Minimum.

N
Número. Number.

O
Onza. Ounce.
Ovalado, -a. Oval.

P
Pendiente. Gradient.
Pie. Foot.
  Pie cuadrado. Square foot.
  Pie cúbito. Cubic foot.
Porcentaje. Percentage
  Por ciento. Percent.
Perspectiva. Perspective.
Peso, pesa. Weight.
Profundidad. Depth.
  Profundo, -a. Deep.

Promedio. Average.
Pulgada. Inch.

R
Rectángulo. Rectangle.
>**Rectangular.** Rectangular.

S
Segmento. Segment.
Sólido, -a. Solid.
Span. Distancia.
Speed. Velocidad.
Superficie. Surface, area.
Simétrico, -a. Symmetrical.

T
Temperatura. Temperature.
Tonelada. Ton.
>**Tonelada métrico.** Metric ton.
Triangular. Triangular.

V
Vertical. Vertical, plumb.
Yarda. Yard.
>**Yarda cuadrada.** Square yard.
>**Yarda cúbita.** Cubic yard.

NÚMEROS/NUMBERS

Uno, 1. One.
Dos, 2. Two.
Tres, 3. Three.
Quatro, 4. Four.
Cinco, 5. Five.
Seis, 6. Six.
Siete, 7. Seven.
Ocho, 8. Eight.
Nueve, 9. Nine.
Diez, 10. Ten.
Once, 11. Eleven.
Doce, 12. Twelve.
Trece, 13. Thirteen.
Catorce, 14. Fourteen.
Quince, 15. Fifteen.
Dieciseis, 16. Sixteen.
Diecisiete, 17. Seventeen.
Dieciocho 18. Eighteen.
Diecinueve, 19. Nineteen.
Veinte, 20. Twenty.
Treinta, 30. Thirty.
Cuarenta, 40. Forty.
Cincuenta, 50. Fifty.
Sesenta, 60. Sixty.
Setenta, 70. Seventy.
Ochenta, 80. Eighty.
Noventa, 90. Ninety.
Cien, ciento, 100. Hundred.
Mil, 1000. Thousand.

Fracciones. Fractions.

Mitad, 1/2. Half.
Tercero, -a., 1/3. Third.

Cuarto, -a. , 1/4. Quarter.
Quinto, -a, 1/5. Fifth.
Sexto, -a., 1/6. Six.
Séptimo, -a., 1/7. Seventh.
Octavo, -a, 1/8. Eighth.
Noveno, -a, 1/9. Ninth.
Decimo, -a. Tenth.
Décimosexto, -a. Sixteenth, 1/16.
Trigésimo-segundo, -a. Thirty-second, 1/32.
Sexagésimo-cuarto, -a. Sixty-fourth, 1/64.

PESTES, PLAGAS Y ENFERMIDADES
PESTS AND DISEASES

A
Ácaro. Mite.
Áfido. Aphid.
Agalla. Gall.
Araña. Spider.
   Telaraña. Spiderweb.
Arañuela. Thrips.
Aruga. Caterpillar.

B
Baba. Slime.
Babosa. Slug.
Broma. Borer, shipworm.

C
Cancro. Canker.
Caracol. Snail.
Clorosis. Chlorosis.
Cochinilla. Slater, woodlice.
Cogollero de maíz. Armyworm.
Colémbolo. Springtail.
Cortadora. Cutworm.
Chapulín. Grasshopper, locust.
Chicharra. Leafhopper.
Chinche. Capsid.

D
Defoliación. Defoliation.
Discoloración. Discoloration.
Enfermidad. Disease.
   Enfermo, -a. Diseased.
Esrosquilla. Earworm.

Escarabajo. Beetle.
Escaladura, escarcha. Frost.

F
Fusarium marchita. Fusarium wilt.

G
Gallina ciega. Grub worm.
Gardama. Armyworm.
Gorgojo. Weevil.
    Gorgojo de algodón. Boll weevil.
    Gorgojo de las raices. Root weevil.
Gusano. Worm.
Gusano cogollero. Armyworm.
Gusano córneo. Hornworm.
Gusano cortador. Cutworm.
    Gusano de elatérido. Wireworm.

H
Halo. Halo.
Hormiga. Ant.
    Hormiga cortadora. Cutter ant.
    Hormigera. Ant hill.
Hongo. Mold, fungus.
Huevo. Egg.

I
Infestación. Infestation, blight, plague.
Infectado, -a. Infected.

L
Langosta. Locust.
Larva. Larvae.
Larva de polilla. Moth larvae.
Lesión. Lesion.

M

Maggot. Larva, cresa.
Mancha. Spot.
Mildiu. Mildew.
Milpiés. Millepede.
Moho, micosis. Fungus, mildew.
    Micótico, -a; fúngico, -a. Fungal.
Moribundo, -a. Moribund.
Mosca. Fly.
Mala hierba, maleza. Weed.
Marchita. Wilt.
    Marchitarse. To wilt.
Mosca o mosquita blanca. Whitefly.
Moteado. Mottling.

N

Nematodo. Nematode.

P

Peste. Pest, plague.
Picudo. Boll weevil.
Plaga. Blight, plague, infestation.
Pulgón. Aphid.

R

Rata. Rat.
Ratón. Mouse.
Roya. Rust, mildew.

S

Saltamontes. Grasshopper.

T

Taltuza, tuza. Gopher.
Tizón. Smut.

V

Verticillium marchita. Verticillium wilt.
Virus. Virus.
Virus mosaico. Mosaic virus.

.

The Spanish-English Dictionary of Gardening and Landscaping is a useful tool for both professionals and homeowners. Flowers, plants and trees; fruits, herbs and vegetables; the garden, greenhouse and nursery; tools, materials and hardware, and much more, all in a categorized, easy-to-read format.

El diccionario español-inglés de jardinería y paisajismo es una herramienta útil para ambos profesionales y propietarios. Flores, plantas y árboles; frutas, hierbas y vegetales; el jardín, el invernadero y el vivero; herramientas, materiales y ferretería, y mucho más, en un formato categorizado y fácil a leer.

COMPILED
BY JAY MISKOWIEC

COVER AND BOOK DESIGN
BY CAROLYN BORGEN

$14.00

51400

9 780982 278482

Ⓐ Aliform Publishing